# INTERACTING
## with Informational
## Text for **CLOSE** and
## **CRITICAL READING**

By Jill Erfourth, Theresa Hasenauer,
and Lorri Zieleniewski

🍎 Maupin House *by*
## capstone
### professional

INTERACTING with Informational Text for CLOSE and CRITICAL READING
By Jill Erfourth, Theresa Hasenauer, and Lorri Zieleniewski

© 2016. Jill Erfourth, Theresa Hasenauer, and Lorri Zieleniewski.

Cover Design: Sandra D'Antonio

Book Design: Jodi Pedersen

Photo Credits: Shutterstock: cover and interior

Websites listed were active and appropriate at the time of publication.

Library of Congress Cataloging-in-Publication Data
Cataloging-in-publication information is on file with the Library of Congress.

978-1-62521-930-5 (pbk.)
978-1-62521-940-4 (ebook PDF)
978-1-4966-0304-3 (ebook)

Maupin House publishes professional resources for K–12 educators.
Contact us for tailored, in-school training or to schedule an author for
a workshop or conference.

Visit www.maupinhouse.com for free lesson plan downloads.

Maupin House Publishing, Inc. by Capstone Professional
1710 Roe Crest Drive
North Mankato, MN 56003

www.maupinhouse.com
888-262-6135
info@maupinhouse.com

# DEDICATION

To my three angels, Keith, Emma, and Donovan
—Jill Erfourth

To my three souls, Ken, Kenny, and Kalvin
—Theresa Hasenauer

To my three hearts, Todd, Roman, and Lola
—Lorri Zieleniewski

# ACKNOWLEDGMENTS

Our sincere thanks to Dr. Elaine Weber for her guidance, patience, and support for the past several years. Her innovation and vision helped to shape the path for this book and its lessons.

A world of gratitude to Melissa Labadie for her expertise in literacy and her contributions to teaching and learning.

# TABLE OF CONTENTS

# FOREWORD

As a teacher or consultant, the greatest reward you can receive is to learn that your work has been useful to those students or teachers receiving it. A still greater reward is that it has not only been found useful, but has been successfully refined and applied in an entirely new context. This is the case with the strategies in this book. The four questions that foster close and critical reading for deeper comprehension and the guided highlighted reading strategy were created for readers in their adolescent years. Over the past five years the authors of this book have adopted, adapted, and embellished these strategies to extend and deepen the comprehension of beginning and developing readers.

The guided highlighted reading strategy is now being used to make the often invisible text structures visible and functioning for the young reader; this application will enhance young readers' ability to read and manage informational text—a skill for the twenty-first century. The authors have also connected the reading work to writing skills. Thanks to the work of these three authors and their colleagues, we have proof that students early in their reading years can read to understand, analyze text for what it says and how it says it, and evaluate text to determine how it supports meaning.

My hope is that the teachers who have been privileged to learn these strategies described and modeled here will apply them to all readers—beginning, developing, and/or advanced. The reward will be for all of us—citizens who know information is everywhere, but when you understand it, analyze it, examine it critically, and think about it deeply to find its lessons, themes, and principles, it becomes knowledge.

> — Dr. Elaine Weber
> Co-author of *Guided Highlighted Reading: A Close Reading Strategy for Navigating Complex Text* and *Reading to the Core: Learning to Read Closely, Critically, and Generatively to Meet Performance Tasks*

# INTRODUCTION

Education today is not the education of your parents' generation or our generation. We live in a time of increasing complexity as we meet the unknown challenges facing our twenty-first-century students. No longer are our students held to a single path or a single fulfilling career in their lifetimes, but an opportunity to continue to grow, change, and diversify their interests. They may change careers as many as 14 times throughout their lives!

This is readily apparent in the shift to the Common Core State Standards (CCSS). These college and career readiness standards were crafted to help students brace for their futures. Through the adoption of CCSS, we seek to prepare our students for the rigorous demands in close and critical reading, writing, thinking, speaking, and listening as they interact daily with text and make strong connections to the world in which we live. Students need to read and think critically as they sift through the layers of meaning when presented with new and complex ideas. Learning and innovation skills are being recognized as the skills students need to prepare for life and work environments in the twenty-first century. A focus on creativity, critical thinking, communication, and collaboration is therefore essential.

## Background and Purpose

What strategies do your students use in order to understand complex text? Read it one time and hope for the best? Read it twice, take a few notes, and move on? Comprehending complex text is, well, complex. CCSS propose that teachers have students interact purposefully with increasingly complex text to build skill and stamina. Fortunately, there are useful strategies and tips that can simplify the process for any student and help him or her effectively understand and apply what was read. We will talk about those strategies in this book and include sample lessons that can be adapted for any book.

What makes text complex? Complexity of text contains three main components: qualitative, quantitative, and reader and task. The qualitative measure of text difficulty is based on levels of meaning, purpose, text structure, features of language, and knowledge demands. The layers of a piece of text become more complex when these elements move from explicit to implicit within the structure. Simple text has a literal message that is brought to the reader's attention with the single or simple purpose of conveying factual information in an explicit and clear way. On the other hand, complex text requires interpretation of text at a deeper level to understand message, theme, and author's purpose. It also requires the understanding of author's craft and why authors have used certain words, phrases, and language within the text. The quantitative measure of text focuses more on word length, word frequency, and sentence length, as measured and generated by a computer. What the reader brings to the task includes experience, knowledge, and motivation, which should be considered in determining whether a text is appropriate. (See Common Core State Standards for ELA Appendix A for more support on text complexity measures.)

We, a collective team of three elementary educators, have found throughout our educational experiences that students need to be reading more closely and analyzing text through multiple readings in order to pull out key information. Just as important, students need to be actively engaged with the text through discussion, purposeful highlighting, note-taking, and responding through writing.

Additionally, we have found that children don't just need more exposure to informational texts, they also need instruction that familiarizes them with each text's organization and structure. "Students who learn to use the organization and structure of informational texts are better able to comprehend and retain the information found in them" (Goldman & Rakestraw, 2000; Pearson & Duke, 2002). Expository text is generally regarded as more difficult than narrative text. Its content can be unfamiliar and frequently represents complex and abstract concepts. There are also many text features to contend with, such as headings, subheadings, captions, graphs, and diagrams. These features can make it challenging for students to organize information and comprehend the content. With continued teacher guidance and practice, students will begin to internalize various expository text structures. This skill is a building block in the development of close and critical reading of complex text. Students can then build on that knowledge to analyze and interpret text to determine inferential meanings, author's purpose, and personal and textual connections. They'll also be able to assimilate new textual information with existing background knowledge to expand their schema.

In addition to providing you with a strategy to hone reading skills, we will also demonstrate how writing can be intertwined throughout close reading to allow students to analyze and reflect on what they are reading. This model, which combines reading and writing, can be used immediately to help students read more critically. Through modeling, scaffolding, and gradual release of instruction, young readers build the habits needed to engage with a complex piece of text. Text, as you will see, doesn't have to be so complex.

## Four Essential Questions of Close and Critical Reading

Teaching students to think critically about text, discuss it, and respond to text is an essential goal of reading and reading instruction. Close and Critical Reading (CCR) is a process that requires students to analyze, synthesize, and respond to increasingly complex text. The guided highlighted reading strategy (Weber, Nelson, Schofield, 2012) encompasses CCR through a four-question framework. Dr. Weber and colleagues are the pioneers of the framework for applying this strategy.

> **Just as important, students need to be actively engaged with the text through discussion, purposeful highlighting, note-taking, and responding through writing.**

"Simply stated, guided highlighted reading (GHR) is a text-based reading strategy that provides explicit support for the close and analytical reading of difficult and complex text in any discipline of study. Teachers choose a short complex text and prepare prompts, generally for one reading purpose at a time. They make copies available to the students and then read each prompt aloud. Students return to the text to find the words and phrases that support their answers" (Weber, Nelson, Schofield, 2012).

This process of the teacher scaffolding text for the students provides access to text that may extend the independent reading level of a student. "GHR is designed to be a temporary scaffold, not an end in itself" (Weber, Nelson, Schofield, 2012). The goal of teacher scaffolding is for the gradual release of responsibility as students acquire the skill of close and critical reading.

With this resource in front of you, you will learn how to implement critical reading strategies in the classroom at the early elementary level using nonfiction complex text, and you will learn how these strategies align with CCSS. You will also see how this strategy is perfect for your at-risk students.

> The goal of teacher scaffolding is for the gradual release of responsibility as students acquire the skill of close and critical reading.

The four essential questions of the CCR Framework take GHR one step further. The questions will help students analyze a text as they read it multiple times and focus on a different purpose during each reading. Scaffolding the student along the way will help them answer the following questions:

1. What does the text say?
2. How does the text say it? (author's craft)
3. What does the text mean? (author's purpose and intent)
4. So what? What does the text mean to me and the world in which I live? (application, evaluation, and integration)

The Four Essential Questions of Close and Critical Reading on page 142 in the Appendix will help you dig in and gain a deeper understanding of close and critical reading while making the connection to the GHR framework.

## Expository Text Structure to Facilitate Comprehension

Expository text offers particular challenges to the reader because abstract and unfamiliar concepts are often presented in an unpredictable organizational pattern. Students should be taught the hierarchical structure of expository text and the interrelationships among ideas—what experts refer to as text structure. "Reading researchers have argued that knowledge of text organization, or structure, is an important factor for text comprehension" (Akhondi, Malayeri, Samad, 2011).
All students, with scaffolding and modeling, can observe the basic organizational pattern of a specific text and look for cues, words, and/or signals to identify which

text structure was actually used by the author. Once the text structure is recognized, students can organize their thinking to match the text. This allows for better comprehension, which in turn can pave the way for writing in that specific text structure. Structural elements in expository texts vary; therefore, it is important to provide students opportunities to experience and become familiar with all five of the most common text structures: description, sequence, compare/contrast, cause/ effect, and problem/solution. Authors of expository texts use these structures to arrange and connect ideas. Akhondi, Malayeri, and Samad (2011) noted, "Students who understand the idea of text structure and how to analyze it are likely to learn more than students who lack this understanding" (p. 368). With this in mind, we provide two GHR lessons for each text structure.

## Guided Highlighted Reading Framework

One of the most significant shifts in education today is the emphasis on critically reading complex text, with a greater focus on informational text. A key requirement of the CCSS for reading is that all students comprehend texts of steadily increasing complexity. The GHR framework supports close and critical reading and provides research-based strategies that align with the 10 Common Core Anchor Standards for Reading. This framework also targets each area of focus that the International Reading Association's Literacy Implementation Guidance for the ELA Common Core State Standards document indicates as possible implementation concerns: use of challenging texts, foundational skills, comprehension, vocabulary, writing, disciplinary literacy, and diverse learners (International Reading Association, 2002).

GHR is interactive, fosters critical thinking, and helps to develop a deep knowledge base for all learners. Can a comprehensive strategy like this be done accurately with early elementary students? Without a doubt! With the GHR framework, elementary teachers truly feel empowered to integrate informational reading comprehension strategies that help students analyze complex text and identify text structures, which will only increase student ability to comprehend text. The GHR framework also allows teachers to build oral language skills as discussion is at the heart of it. At the K–1 level, students can engage with complex texts to support language development and emerging comprehension skills. This builds oral language development and the skills needed to interact with more complex text at the second- and third-grade levels.

Embedded within the framework are research-based strategies, including vocabulary development, text structure analysis, and informational writing. This model and framework meets the needs of all learners at all levels, as teachers begin the process with scaffolding to aid in the gradual release of responsibility.

**The GHR framework also allows teachers to build oral language skills as discussion is at the heart of it.**

## Bridging Expository Reading with Writing

Reading, speaking, and listening should be used as a launching pad for writing pieces. Responding to reading requires students to synthesize information from a text and cite text evidence in order to gain insight, reveal their thinking, and interact with text in meaningful ways. Young students need to see and hear examples of good writing pieces, and teachers need to explicitly point out examples within text. Often teachers can demonstrate this through the use of quality mentor texts. GHR will strengthen student ability to make connections and demonstrate understanding in their own writing.

Taking into consideration the expectations of CCSS, students need to write informative/explanatory pieces to examine and convey complex ideas and information clearly and accurately through the effective selection, organization, and analysis of content. We developed paragraph frames (starting on Appendix p. 129) that help students cite specific text evidence in order to support writing in an organized, scaffolded format. Students can then use the information they highlighted during instruction, along with the paragraph frames, to respond in writing to a text.

## Organization of the Lessons and Instructional Routine

We have organized the lessons in a user-friendly format that will allow any teacher to begin implementing them immediately in the classroom. The next section will walk you through a GHR lesson. Pages 18–23 include a sample routine.

### Preparing for the Lessons

This book includes 10 texts, using a GHR framework, to promote close and critical reading. We provide each passage in the Appendix, which we recommend photocopying for students so that they can highlight the text as you read the prompts. As a scaffold for kindergarten and first-grade students, another option could be to gather at an area of the classroom, perhaps in front of a whiteboard, digital media display, or chart paper, to do the highlighting process together.

The lessons are grouped by text structure: sequencing, description, compare/contrast, cause/effect, and problem/solution. We give a grade span for each passage, but you may find that, depending on your students' needs, you need to dip below the grade level you teach or select a passage that is at a higher level.

The lessons focus on the four essential questions of the CCR Framework. Days 1 and 2 are devoted to specific highlighting activities, so you will need to set aside a day for each activity. For Day 3, you will have a conversation with students about the author's message and connection to text, self, and world. Day 4 is for extended thinking activities and writing extensions. By reading the text for a different purpose each day, students gain a better understanding of the central message. We have included teacher-led guided prompts for highlighting the text.

Here is the focus by day.

| DAY 1: Question 1 Restatement of the Text<br><br>Q1: What does the text say? | DAY 2: Question 2 Description and Author's Craft<br><br>Q2: How does the text say it? | DAY 3: Question 3 Interpretation of Author's Purpose and Intent<br><br>Q3: What does the text mean? | DAY 3: Question 4 Application, Evaluation, and Integration<br><br>Q4: So what? What does the text mean in your life and/or in the lives of others? | DAY 4: Optional Extended Thinking Activities and Writing Extensions |
|---|---|---|---|---|
| Students will read and discuss the literal (surface) level of the text using the main points and logical inferences. This may include facts, claims, or the message or universal theme that can be proven with explicit evidence from the text. | Students will read and discuss the author's craft and purpose, including the techniques good writers use when writing and text structures. Students look specifically at common text structures, genre, organizations, text features, word choice, figures of speech, punctuation, and formatting. | Students will discuss the author's purpose and intent, what the theme/ message is, and how the author's choices facilitate achieving this purpose. They will be responding to questions about what the author wants the reader to believe and what the universal theme of the text is. | Students will read and discuss the text in relationship to their lives and make connections with the world in which we live. They will make text-to-self, text-to-text, and text-to-world connections. | **Extended Thinking Activities:** Students will apply and synthesize knowledge obtained through the close and critical reading process.<br><br>**Writing Extensions:** Students will apply their knowledge of what they read in a written format. They will provide text evidence and cite from a source. |

Before you begin a lesson, think about what time of the day would work best for your students, and set aside 20–30 minutes. Each lesson takes approximately four days to complete, including responding to reading. Planning the lesson using consecutive days will support the scaffolding process. Listed below are some additional tools you might need to get started:

- Chart paper
- Colored markers/highlighters
- Highlighter tape
- Word pointers/word highlighters
- Pipe cleaners to highlight words
- Vocabulary word wall/note cards
- Interactive whiteboard
- Document camera
- Student versions of the passages (available in the Appendix, starting on page 104)

The lessons begin with these important parts in order to build content knowledge.

## Background Knowledge

Teachers have been moving away from providing excessive amounts of background knowledge. At K–3, however, it might be necessary to provide more information and more support to help students begin to access complex text. To develop appropriate background knowledge, topics and vocabulary are introduced. This helps engage students for further learning. For kindergarten and first-grade students, the background knowledge may need more scaffolding, such as with discussion prompts. Second- and third-grade students will have less scaffolding as they have more prior knowledge.

## Anticipatory Set

Days 1 and 2 of a lesson include an anticipatory set. An anticipatory set is a brief activity that captures your audience's attention and allows them to become engaged in the subject being taught or focused upon. This brief activity encourages oral discussion as it includes authentic questions that are generative in nature. "That is, they generate or help to promote class inquiry and discovery, framing learning as a complex, multifaceted, communal activity as opposed to a process of simply accumulating information" (Ritchhart, Church, Morrison, 2011).

With each GHR lesson in this book, we provide directions to a video clip that students can watch and respond to in collaborative discussion. Using video clips not only provides practice with the video responses on new state assessments, such as the Smarter Balanced Assessment, but they also help harness and capture the attention of your young learners and build background knowledge. Websites for video clips listed were active and appropriate at the time of publication. You may also consider using books and/or book excerpts for a powerful anticipatory set. From these specific pieces of text, collaborative and teacher-led discussion can take place. Photographs, specific objects that the students can pass around and touch, quick journal writing, and leading questions can also prove to be powerful in setting the stage for the GHR lesson.

When using the videos, it is recommended that you pull them up before class and increase the size of the videos to a full screen so students do not see any user comments.

## Vocabulary

Often students have difficulty with the vocabulary of a given piece of complex text. More explicit instruction with specific words and word meanings is necessary to scaffold complex text for students. As developed by Isabel Beck and colleagues (2002, 2008), words are classified into three separate tiers. Tier 1 includes the most basic words used in everyday speech and are usually learned in the early grades. Tier 2 words are also basic words, but they are process oriented, fundamental to comprehension, and should be explicitly taught. Tier 3 words are low-frequency, domain-specific words that are relevant to comprehension to that particular text.

### Tiered Vocabulary Examples

| Tier 1 | Tier 2 | Tier 3 |
|---|---|---|
| book, girl, sad, do, orange | fortunate, surface, measure, separate | igneous, legal, peninsula |

Prior to the first reading of a text, focus should be placed on vocabulary words that may interfere with the overall understanding and key ideas of the text. These could be Tier 2 or Tier 3 words. We call out specific words from the text for brief, explicit instruction and give suggestions on Days 1 and 2 on how to introduce these words or review them.

## Accommodations

Every classroom has learners who require approaches that differ from your standard routine. Special education students, at-risk children, and English language learners will need additional scaffolding to help them access the text and be successful.

Before you begin your actual GHR lesson, have your at-risk students in mind. These students will need additional scaffolding provided by you so they will have equal access to complex text. You can scaffold lessons by having collaborative discussions in small groups, using additional visuals or models, pre-teaching challenging vocabulary, and explicitly teaching specific complexities of the text, which may include sentence structure, literary devices, and so on.

You can also differentiate your GHR lessons to meet the needs of students. GHR is the perfect strategy because it lends itself to accommodating each student in a way that is necessary for success and allows equal access to complex text and the standards. To accommodate appropriately and effectively, it is suggested that you read the text before you share it with students. This way, you can identify items that may cause confusion, such as a complex sentence. You can then discuss complex sentences in small groups prior to the whole-group lesson. By providing this scaffolding, you are allowing students equal access to complex text. Initially the text may be challenging for students, however with scaffolding and teacher support the students will move toward independence.

The next few pages show how a lesson will flow. We have included support in each part to promote discussion. As needed, provide additional scaffolds to support your students.

# INSTRUCTIONAL ROUTINE: Sample Lesson
## DAY 1: Q1: What does the text say?—Surface Read

CCSS.ELA-LITERACY.CCRA.R.1, CCSS.ELA-LITERACY.CCRA.R.2, CCSS.ELA-LITERACY.CCRA.R.3

## Background Knowledge

This is your opportunity to introduce the topic and/or present leading discussion questions to set background knowledge. It is important to give early elementary students background knowledge so they can discuss the text, understand it, and access it appropriately.

## Anticipatory Set

Use discussion questions and multimedia, such as video clips, links to photos, podcasts, music, pictures, discussion prompts, etc. to set the purpose and engage students. We have provided directions to video links, but you may decide to use something else. Also provided are discussion questions and prompts.

## Vocabulary

The lessons include specific vocabulary with definitions. On Day 1 of the lesson, we provide Tier 2 and Tier 3 words that may interfere with the overall complexity and key ideas of that particular text. It is then recommended that you provide explicit instruction on these words, such as with the following activities:

• Give a student-friendly definition of the word using an online dictionary as a resource. We have provided this definition.

• Add words to a visual word bank that can be created in the front of the class on an easel or on chart paper.

• Chant or cheer the words three to five times, pronouncing them accurately each time.

• Give students an oral example of how the word is used and relate it to something they already know.

## Directions for Teacher-guided Prompts for Highlighting Text

During this part, you will read the text with students and provide scaffolding as needed. Grade-specific directions are included with each lesson. This happens accordingly:

1. Prior to Day 1, photocopy the text from the Appendix. Work with students in a whole-group setting with one enlarged copy of the text displayed on a whiteboard where you model how to highlight specific information. Depending on ability, students can either interact with the enlarged text at the whiteboard with teacher-supplied tools (e.g., highlighter tape, magnifying glasses, pointers, word-framing tools) or their own photocopy of the text. Record the highlighted responses on the enlarged version as needed.

2. Read the text out loud. Students can choral/echo read the text based on their instructional needs.

3. Before reading the prompts, explain to students that the first day of reading the text and highlighting the key ideas and details will lead to a summary of the text.

4. Either read the text in its entirety and then read the GHR prompts, or read the text line by line. Guide students to find the words to highlight by listening carefully to the words in the prompts, which contain words from the text.

# INSTRUCTIONAL ROUTINE: Sample Lesson
## DAY 1: Teacher-led Highlight Prompts

Read the prompts prepared for each paragraph or sentence. Students then scan the designated area to highlight the specific text related to the prompt. It's recommended that students in grades K–1 work in a whole group with one enlarged copy of the text on chart paper and/or displayed on a whiteboard where you model how to highlight specific information. Students can interact with the enlarged text by coming up to the chart paper or whiteboard using highlighter tape, magnifying glasses, word-framing tools, etc.

## Text
This is where the passage will appear.

## Q1: What does the text say?—Surface Read
Teacher-led prompts for highlighting the text will appear here.

We include specific directions on what and where to highlight. These prompts help answer Question 1 and will help students create a summary of the passage. As you read the prompts out loud, students scan the text for the correct answer. (Scanning may not be an option at grades K–1. The K–1 lessons suggest choosing a highlighting method for you to model highlighting in a group setting. Students then interact with the text in a variety of ways, such as mimicking you by using highlighter tape on the same words that you highlighted.)

It is suggested that for the first few times, students who know the answer raise their hands, you select one student to respond, and all hear the correct answer and highlight together before allowing students to highlight on their own. The purpose is for students to learn how to identify key ideas and details to build a one- to two-sentence summary of a passage.

## Question 1 Discussion and Summary: What does the text say?

Summarizing teaches students how to discern the most important ideas in a text and how to integrate the central ideas in a meaningful way. After students have completed highlighting the prompts, have them look over all of the words they have highlighted. Review prompts and discuss why they think those specific words were highlighted. Use some of the highlighted words to create a word bank, which we have included in each lesson. Then model a summary of the passage using several of the words from the word bank. For grades K–1, this can be done using the summary frame provided in each lesson. Depending on the level of your students, it may be necessary to provide additional scaffolding and modeling of a summary.

For students in grades 2–3, a respond-to-reading activity is included in the Appendix that can be used for each lesson. After collaborative discussion, students can respond to each of the four questions in written format to bridge close and critical reading with writing. As students move to independence, they can write their response independently.

## Example Activity to Help Scaffold for Summary

Using a sentence frame, students in grades K–1 will complete a one-sentence summary. For example:

This _____ (genre) article is about _____ (topic, theme, gist, big idea) and _____ (a connection to the topic, theme, gist, big idea).

CCSS.ELA-LITERACY.CCRA.R.4, CCSS.ELA-LITERACY.CCRA.R.5, CCSS.ELA-LITERACY.CCRA.R.6

## Review Summary from Day 1

Revisit the summaries the students generated on Day 1.

## Anticipatory Set

Revisit the Anticipatory Set from Day 1 to re-engage students and set the purpose for close reading of the text. After watching the video, discuss what was learned from the video.

### Video Discussion

Video discussion prompt will appear here.

## Vocabulary Day 2

On Day 2 of the lesson, the focus of this part of the instruction is to build and enhance students' vocabulary. Review vocabulary words from Day 1. Choose one or more of the following activities to reinforce vocabulary:

• Create a visual presentation using the vocabulary terms.

• Present words in a graphic organizer, such as a Frayer Model.

• Make a headline for one of the vocabulary words as if it were a newspaper or an online article.

• Use one vocabulary word to create shades of meaning cards.

• Use the word in a metaphor with students, or have them come up with their own metaphors.

• For more specific vocabulary instruction, refer to Marzano's Six-Step Process for Vocabulary Instruction: providing a description, giving an explanation or example of the new term, restating the definition in the student's own words, creating a picture, engaging in specific activities and discussing the terms with other students in class, and involving the words in games so students can play with the terms.

## Q2: How does the text say it?

On Day 2, you will conduct a close reading of the text for deeper meaning. This will include identifying the text structure, text features, author's craft, word choice, and author's style. Understanding these elements of the text will help strengthen comprehension and bring awareness to the author's message and theme.

## Directions for Teacher-guided Prompts for Highlighting Text

1. Read the text out loud.

2. Choose a different color highlighter for Day 2.

3. Before reading the prompts to students, explain that the second read is to answer Q2: How does the text say it? They will look at the text through a different lens. This time they'll look at the text for a deeper meaning and discuss how the author wrote the text.

Explain that authors intentionally use words and author's craft to convey their message and purpose for the text.

4. Either read the text in its entirety and then read the prompts for highlighting, or read the text line by line, and have students highlight the text after each line is read aloud. It can be done either way depending on the level of your students. Guide students to find the word(s) in the text to highlight.

# INSTRUCTIONAL ROUTINE: Sample Lesson
## DAY 2: Teacher-led Highlight Prompts

Read the prompts prepared for each paragraph or sentence. Students then scan the designated area to highlight the specific text related to the prompt. It's recommended that students in grades K–1 work in a whole group with one enlarged copy of the text on chart paper and/or displayed on a whiteboard where you model how to highlight specific information. Students can interact with the enlarged text by coming up to the chart paper or whiteboard using highlighter tape, magnifying glasses, word-framing tools, etc.

## Text Passage

This is where the passage will appear.

## Q2: How does the text say it?—Close Read

Teacher-led prompts for highlighting the text will appear here.

We include specific directions on what and where to highlight. These prompts help answer Question 2 and guide students to understand how the author wrote the text using specific words, phrases, and language. As you read the prompts out loud, students scan the text for the correct answer.

It is suggested that for the first few times, students who know the answer raise their hands, you select one student to respond, and all hear the correct answer and highlight together before allowing students to highlight on their own. The purpose is for students to learn how to pick out key ideas and details to build a one- to two-sentence summary of a passage, with author's craft in mind.

## Question 2 Discussion: How does the text say it?

After students have completed highlighting the prompts, discuss with students how the author wrote the text using specific word choice, figurative language, organization, text features, imagery, writing techniques, and even the tone of the piece.

In the lessons, we focused on a few of the elements mentioned above. The expectation is not necessarily to cover every element of Question 2 for every text that is read. Use your professional judgment as to which elements are important to focus on. You may choose to elaborate further on Question 2 than the lessons suggest in this book.

# INSTRUCTIONAL ROUTINE: Sample Lesson
## DAY 3: Q3: What does the text mean?—Interpret Text/Critical Thinking

CCSS.ELA-LITERACY.CCRA.R.8

On this day, you will review what students have highlighted for Questions 1 and 2, and consider the meaning of the text through a discussion/reflection format. Then you will guide the students to consider the meaning of the text and what the author's purpose was in writing the text. Asking what the text means transitions students from focusing on literal questions to relying more on inferences. When students make inferences, they must consider what is implied and understand the author's purpose. During this part of the lesson, students reflect on the first two questions (What does the text say? How does the text say it?) to analyze parts of the text and integrate that knowledge to consider the meaning of the whole text.

## DAY 3: Q4: What does it mean to my life?—Applications and Connections

CCSS.ELA-LITERACY.CCRA.R.9

After interacting with the text to answer Questions 1, 2, and 3, students will consider the meaning of text as it applies to themselves, other texts, and the world around them. Making these text-to-self, text-to-text, and text-to-world connections will deepen students' understanding of the text.

# INSTRUCTIONAL ROUTINE: Sample Lesson
## DAY 4:

## Extended Thinking Activities to Apply and Synthesize Text

The purpose of these activities is to apply and synthesize knowledge obtained through the close and critical reading process. The activities help to solidify comprehension and allow students to demonstrate what they learned through the critical reading process.

## Writing Extensions

Through writing extensions, students can apply their knowledge of what they read in a written format. The extensions allow students to provide text evidence and even cite from a source. The writing frames provide focus on each specific text structure and help students apply their knowledge in an appropriate, scaffolded format. In addition, extensions provide an opportunity to write a new piece using the text structure studied. Consider using these writing extensions as an assessment of students' understanding of the text and of the text structure.

# LESSONS FOR SEQUENCING TEXT STRUCTURE

CCSS.ELA-LITERACY.CCRA.R.1, CCSS.ELA-LITERACY.CCRA.R.2, CCSS.ELA-LITERACY.CCRA.R.3

Build the context for the reading by activating prior knowledge using the following:

## Background Knowledge

Say: *Recycling is using something in a new way. Recycling is important to our Earth.*

## Anticipatory Set

Before you start the session, go to YouTube and search for "Let's Go Green Kids: 'Recycle It.'" Enlarge the video to the size of your screen, and watch it with students. Use the discussion stems below to have a brief conversation about the video with students.

### Video Discussion

• Name one thing that the video said can be recycled. (Sunday paper, soup can, jar, gum wrapper)

• Name something made of plastic that can be recycled. (Plastic bag)

• What do they tell you to do with a soup can? (Recycle it)

## Vocabulary

Explicitly teach the vocabulary words from the text. Use one or more of the suggested activities, which are meant to be direct and brief:

• Give a student-friendly definition of the word using an online dictionary as a resource. We have provided this definition.

• Add words to a visual word bank that can be created in the front of the class, on an easel, or on chart paper.

• Chant or cheer the words three to five times, pronouncing them accurately each time.

• Give students an oral example of how the word is used and relate it to something they already know.

**bin:** a container or box used to put things in
**factory:** a building where something is made
**melt:** to change from a solid to a liquid
**sorted:** to put things in a group
**recycled:** used again

## Directions for Teacher-guided Prompts for Highlighting Text

1. Prior to Day 1, create an enlarged copy of the text so you can model how to highlight specific information. Depending on student ability, students can either interact with the enlarged text (using the tools referenced on page 15) or, if appropriate, their own copies of the text. Choose one color to highlight responses to the prompts.

2. Read the text out loud. Students can choral/echo read the text based on their instructional needs.

3. Before reading the prompts, explain to students that the first day of reading the text and highlighting the key ideas and details will lead to a summary of the text.

4. Either read the text in its entirety and then read the GHR prompts, or read the text line by line. Guide students to find the words to highlight by listening carefully to the words in the prompts, which contain words from the text.

# LESSON 1: How Plastic Is Recycled, Grades K–1
## DAY 1: Teacher-led Highlight Prompts

### How Plastic Is Recycled

**P1** Things made of plastic can be recycled. They can be made into something new.

**P2** People put plastic into bins. Workers take the plastic to a factory. The plastic is sorted. It is washed. Then it is chopped. The pieces are dried. They are heated and they melt. Finally, they are put into water to cool.

**P3** Now the plastic is new again! It can be used to make new things.

**Paragraph 1:** Highlight what can be done with things made of plastic.

**Paragraph 1:** Highlight what plastic can be made into.

**Paragraph 2:** Highlight what people put plastic into.

**Paragraph 2:** Highlight where workers take the plastic.

**Paragraph 2:** Highlight the first thing that happens to the plastic.

**Paragraph 2:** Highlight what happens after the pieces are heated.

**Paragraph 2:** Highlight what they are put into to cool.

**Paragraph 3:** Highlight what is new again.

**Paragraph 3:** Highlight what the plastic can be used to make.

## Question 1 Discussion and Summary: What does the text say?

Encourage students to turn and talk with a partner about what they highlighted and why they think these are the key ideas or important pieces of information in the text. Then display the words below on a board or on chart paper. Ask students to review the words and use them to complete the sentence frame summary. Guide and scaffold students with this activity as needed.

### Summary Word Bank
**new, plastic, recycled**

This informational text is about _____ .

(This informational text is about the steps of how plastic is recycled.)

CCSS.ELA-LITERACY.CCRA.R.4, CCSS.ELA-LITERACY.CCRA.R.5, CCSS.ELA-LITERACY.CCRA.R.6

## Review Summary from Day 1

Revisit the summaries the students generated on Day 1.

## Anticipatory Set

Re-engage students on Day 2 with a second viewing of the video. After viewing the video, use the sentence frame to have students turn and talk with a partner and share one thing they learned from the video.

## Video Discussion

In the video about _____ , I learned _____ .

## Vocabulary Day 2

In order to scaffold the text for all students, vocabulary is revisited and a more in-depth analysis of the words is conducted. You can choose from one or more of the following activities to reinforce and expand vocabulary development.

- Create a visual presentation using the vocabulary terms.
- Present words in a graphic organizer, such as a Frayer Model.
- Make a headline for one of the vocabulary words as if it were a newspaper or an online article.
- Use one vocabulary word to create shades of meaning cards.
- Use the word in a metaphor with students, or have them come up with their own metaphors.

- For more specific vocabulary instruction, refer to Marzano's Six-Step Process for Vocabulary Instruction: providing a description, giving an explanation or example of the new term, restating the definition in the student's own words, creating a picture, engaging in specific activities and discussing the terms with other students in class, and involving the words in games so students can play with the terms.

**bin:** a container or box used to put things in
**factory:** a building where something is made
**melt:** to change from a solid to a liquid
**sorted:** to put things in a group
**recycled:** used again

## Teacher-led Summary for Q2: How does the text say it?

This is a teacher-led summary that can be removed as students become more independent in identifying the text structure, author's craft, and text features.

Say: *This informational article has a text structure that shows events in the order that they happened, or sequence. This sequence structure is about the process of recycling plastic. Signal words help identify this text structure, such as "then" and "finally."*

## Directions for Teacher-guided Prompts for Highlighting Text

1. Use a different color to highlight the text on Day 2. Use the same highlighting method as Day 1.

2. Before reading the prompts to students, explain that the second read is to answer Q2: How does the text say it? This time they'll look at the text for a deeper meaning and discuss how the author wrote the text. You will want to point out to students that authors are purposeful when they write.

3. Either read the text in its entirety and then read the prompts for highlighting, or read the text line by line and have students highlight the text after each line is read aloud.

4. Read prompts for students to highlight the answers in the text. Guide students to find the word(s) in the text to highlight.

**T** **How Plastic Is Recycled**

Published by ReadWorks.org: The Solution to Reading Comprehension. © 2013 ReadWorks®, Inc.
All rights reserved.

**P1** Things made of plastic can be recycled. They can be made into something new.

**P2** People put plastic into bins. Workers take the plastic to a factory. The plastic is sorted. It is washed. Then it is chopped. The pieces are dried. They are heated and they melt. Finally, they are put into water to cool.

**P3** Now the plastic is new again! It can be used to make new things.

**Title:** Highlight the title.

**Paragraph 2:** Highlight the people who take the plastic to the factory.

**Paragraph 2:** Highlight the word that tells you what step comes next.

**Paragraph 2:** Highlight the word that tells you the final step is coming.

**Paragraph 3:** Highlight the punctuation mark that shows excitement.

## Question 2 Discussion: How does the text say it?

After highlighting the text for Question 2, discuss with students the techniques of craft and structure the author uses in the text, which is what they have highlighted. When you begin this discussion, you will need to provide scaffolding until students are able to identify these elements independently.

Below are the elements to discuss with students to answer Question 2: How does the text say it?

## Text Structure

Say: *The text structure is sequence. How do we know this is a sequence text structure?* (The text includes events in the order that they happen.) *What signal words did we highlight to show there is a sequence of recycling?* (Then, Finally)

## Author's Craft

Say: *The author uses an exclamation point to show emotion about how items can be used again. How do you think the author feels at the end of this text?* (Answers may include: The author feels it's important to recycle and wants the reader to know about recycling plastic.)

# LESSON 1: How Plastic Is Recycled, Grades K–1
## DAY 3: Q3: What does the text mean?—Interpret Text/Critical Thinking

CCSS.ELA-LITERACY.CCRA.R.8

Review all the guided highlights from Questions 1 and 2, and consider the meaning of the text through discussion. Guide students to interpret the text by considering the meaning of the text. This discussion may need to be scaffolded, depending on student ability.

Say: *The message of this text is that items we use in everyday life can be used again and again.*

Guide a discussion with students to understand the author's purpose in writing this text. Help students make an inference from the text they read and what they have highlighted. Through collaborative conversation, students may have varied interpretations of the author's purpose for writing the text.

Say: *Why do you think the author wants you to know about how things are recycled?* Wait for students to respond, and then say: *The author may want us to know how things can be recycled so we can do our part to reuse items and not create waste. This will help protect our Earth and environment.*

## DAY 3: Q4: What does it mean to my life?—Applications and Connections

CCSS.ELA-LITERACY.CCRA.R.9

Guide students in making connections. By making connections, students are able to have a deeper understanding of what they read.

**Text-to-text:** Ask students to relate this text to other passages or books about recycling. If necessary, show text that has been previously read about recycling and ask students to identify similarities and/or differences.

**Text-to-self:** Discuss the following questions with students. You can have them turn and talk with a partner or share as a group.

• *Do you recycle at home?* (Yes)

• *What are some things you can do at home to help recycle?* (Sort plastic bottles, milk cartons/jugs, etc. into separate recycling bins)

• *What types of things do you use at home and school that can be recycled?* (Paper, bags, water bottles)

**Text-to-world:** Discuss the following questions with students. You can have them turn and talk with a partner or share as a group.

• *Why do we recycle?* (To help our world stay clean, to reduce the amount of waste, and so we can make new things)

• *What would happen if we didn't recycle?* (More garbage and waste/pollution would be everywhere.)

• *Where might all of the garbage go?* (In our lakes, rivers, oceans, and landfills, etc.)

## Extended Thinking Activities to Apply and Synthesize Text

- Have students complete the How Plastic Is Recycled Sequence Graphic Organizer on page 107.

- Make a craft (like a new toy, robot, pencil holder, etc.) with recycled plastic, cardboard, or cans. Make sure that recycled cans do not contain any sharp edges.

- Get a recycle bin for your classroom, and put waste paper, plastic, and cardboard in it. Take it to a recycle center.

## Writing Extensions

- You may choose to complete the How Plastic Is Recycled Sequence Graphic Organizer from the Extended Thinking Activities. Then have students use this to assist in completing the Sequencing Paragraph Frame on page 135.

- You can explicitly teach students how to write an expository sequence text using the Sequencing Paragraph Frame. Model and scaffold the paragraph frame with students until they can do it independently.

- Encourage students to apply the text structure to another writing format, such as a poster promoting recyling.

# LESSON 2: Life Story of a Butterfly, Grades 2–3

**DAY 1: Q1: What does the text say?—Surface Read**

Text, pp. 108–110

CCSS.ELA-LITERACY.CCRA.R.1, CCSS.ELA-LITERACY.CCRA.R.2, CCSS.ELA-LITERACY.CCRA.R.3

Build the context for the reading by activating prior knowledge using the following:

## Background Knowledge

Say: *Butterflies are adult caterpillars. Caterpillars go through many changes before becoming a butterfly.*

## Anticipatory Set

Before you start the session, search for "National Geographic Channel" and "Growing Up Butterfly" in a search engine. Enlarge the video to the size of your screen, and watch it with students. Use the discussion stems below to have a brief conversation with the students about the video.

## Video Discussion

- What kind of animal is a butterfly? (An insect)

- Are a caterpillar and a butterfly the same kind of animal? (Yes)

- What were some of the changes the caterpillar went through? (Egg, caterpillar, chrysalis, butterfly)

## Vocabulary

Explicitly teach the vocabulary words from the text. Use one or more of the suggested activities, which are meant to be direct and brief:

- Give a student-friendly definition of the word using an online dictionary as a resource. We have provided this definition.

- Add words to a visual word bank that can be created in the front of the class, on an easel, or on chart paper.

- Chant or cheer the words three to five times, pronouncing them accurately each time.

- Give students an oral example of how the word is used and relate it to something they already know.

**larva:** a young form of an insect that looks like a worm
**metamorphosis:** stages in which an animal changes body shape and appearance
**pale:** light in color
**pupa:** an insect in the stage between larva and adult; for a butterfly, this is when it's in a chrysalis
**shell:** a hard outer covering
**splits:** breaks apart

## Directions for Teacher-guided Prompts for Highlighting Text

1. Prior to Day 1, photocopy the text passage from the Appendix for each student. Work with students in a whole-group setting with one enlarged copy of the displayed text so you can model how to highlight specific information. Students will choose one color to highlight their responses to the prompts.

2. Read the text out loud. Students can choral/echo read the text based on their instructional needs.

3. Before reading the prompts, explain to students that the first day of reading the text and highlighting the key ideas and details will lead to a summary of the text.

4. Either read the text in its entirety and then read the GHR prompts, or read the text line by line. Guide students to find the words to highlight by listening carefully to the words in the prompts, which contain words from the text.

LIFE STORY OF A BUTTERFLY • LESSON 2

## Life Story of a Butterfly

By Charlotte Guillain, published by Heinemann-Raintree

**P1**

### What Is a Butterfly?

A butterfly is a type of animal called an insect. Insects are animals with three pairs of legs and a body with three main parts. Many insects have wings. There are many types of butterflies. They live in many places around the world and can be different sizes and colors.

**P2**

### A Butterfly's Life Story

Like all other animals, a butterfly goes through different stages as it grows into an adult. These stages make up an animal's life story. Follow the life story of butterflies, and watch them change in unusual ways as they develop and grow.

**P3**

### It Starts with an Egg

A butterfly starts its life as an egg. The egg is oval shaped, tiny, and white. A butterfly's mother usually lays one egg under a leaf. A sticky substance holds the egg onto the plant.

**P4**

### The Egg Hatches

After three to five days, the larva starts to hatch from the egg. A butterfly larva is usually called a caterpillar. This tiny caterpillar is pale, with a dark head to start with. As it grows it changes color.

**P5**

### A Growing Caterpillar

The caterpillar starts to eat. First it eats its own egg, and then it starts to feed on the plants around it. It gets bigger and bigger. The caterpillar grows so much that its skin splits several times. When its skin splits, the caterpillar crawls out with a soft new skin.

**Paragraph 1:** Highlight what type of animal a butterfly is.

**Paragraph 1:** Highlight what there are many types of.

**Paragraph 1:** Highlight where butterflies live.

**Paragraph 1:** Highlight what can be different about butterflies.

**Paragraph 2:** Highlight what butterflies go through.

**Paragraph 2:** Highlight what the stages make up.

**Heading for Paragraph 3:** Highlight what it starts with.

**Paragraph 3:** Highlight where the mother butterfly lays her egg.

**Paragraph 4:** Highlight what starts to hatch after three to five days.

**Paragraph 4:** Highlight what the larva is usually called.

**Paragraph 5:** Highlight what the caterpillar eats first.

**Paragraph 5:** Highlight what the caterpillar crawls out with after its skin splits.

— CONTINUED

### Changing into a Pupa

**P6** When a caterpillar is very fat, it cannot grow any bigger. It makes a sticky liquid and attaches itself to a twig or leaf. The caterpillar's skin splits one more time. A pupa is now underneath. The pupa has a hard shell. A pupa is sometimes called a chrysalis. The stage when a caterpillar changes into an adult is called a pupa. This change of body shape is called metamorphosis. It takes a monarch butterfly about 10 days to turn into an adult. Other butterflies can take months to change into adults.

**Paragraph 6:** Highlight what the caterpillar attaches itself to.

**Paragraph 6:** Highlight what a pupa is sometimes called.

**Paragraph 6:** Highlight what the change of body shape is called.

### Changing into an Adult

**P7** When a pupa has changed into an adult butterfly, the shell around it splits open. It slowly comes out of the shell. The adult butterfly's wings are soft and damp at first. It has to wait a few hours for its wings to dry and its body to get harder. Like all insects, an adult butterfly has three body parts. These are the head, the thorax, and the abdomen. On a butterfly's head there are two eyes and two antennae, which it uses to smell food. In its mouth is a long tube called a proboscis, which it uses to suck up food.

**Paragraph 7:** Highlight what the three body parts are.

**Paragraph 7:** Highlight what a butterfly's head has two each of.

### Mating

**P8** The butterfly looks for a mate, so they can continue the life story. Together they can reproduce and create new butterflies.

**Paragraph 8:** Highlight what a butterfly looks for.

**Paragraph 8:** Highlight what butterflies can create.

## Question 1 Discussion and Summary: What does the text say?

Encourage students to turn and talk with a partner about what they highlighted and why they think these are the key ideas or important pieces of information in the text. Create a word bank on chart paper or displayed on a whiteboard using the words below to guide students to a summary. Scaffold students with this activity as needed.

As students move to independence, they can write a summary under Q1: What does the text say? on the Respond to Reading page. (See Appendix, p. 140.)

### Summary Word Bank

**butterflies, caterpillar, chrysalis, egg, larva, life story, pupa, stages**

CCSS.ELA-LITERACY.CCRA.R.4, CCSS.ELA-LITERACY.CCRA.R.5, CCSS.ELA-LITERACY.CCRA.R.6

## Review Summary from Day 1

Revisit the summaries the students generated on Day 1.

## Anticipatory Set

Re-engage students on Day 2 with a second viewing of the video. After viewing the video, use the sentence frame to have students turn and talk with a partner and share one thing they learned from the video.

## Video Discussion

In the video about _____ , I learned _____ .

## Vocabulary Day 2

In order to scaffold the text for all students, vocabulary is revisited and a more in-depth analysis of the words is conducted. You can choose from one or more of the following activities to reinforce and expand vocabulary development.

- Create a visual presentation using the vocabulary terms.
- Present words in a graphic organizer, such as a Frayer Model.
- Make a headline for one of the vocabulary words as if it were a newspaper or an online article.
- Use one vocabulary word to create shades of meaning cards.
- Use the word in a metaphor with students, or have them come up with their own metaphors.
- For more specific vocabulary instruction, Refer to Marzano's Six-Step Process for Vocabulary Instruction:

providing a description, giving an explanation or example of the new term, restating the definition in the student's own words, creating a picture, engaging in specific activities and discussing the terms with other students in class, and involving the words in games so students can play with the terms.

**larva:** a young form of an insect that looks like a worm
**metamorphosis:** stages in which an animal changes body shape and appearance
**pale:** light in color
**pupa:** an insect in the stage between larva and adult; for a butterfly, this is when it's in a chrysalis
**shell:** a hard outer covering
**splits:** breaks apart

## Teacher-led Summary for Q2: How does the text say it?

This teacher-led summary can be removed as students become more independent in identifying the text structure, author's craft, and text features.

Say: *This informational text is organized by sequence. The passage uses the signal words "first," "then," "after," and "one more time." The author also uses descriptive words to help visualize the butterfly.*

## Directions for Teacher-guided Prompts for Highlighting Text

1. Read the text out loud.
2. Choose a different color highlighter for Day 2.
3. Before reading the prompts to students, explain that the second read is to answer Q2: How does the text say it? They will look at the text through a different lens. This time they'll look at the text for a deeper meaning and discuss how the author wrote the text. Explain that

authors intentionally use words and author's craft to convey their message and purpose for the text.

4. Either read the text in its entirety and then read the prompts for highlighting, or read the text line by line. Guide students to find the words to highlight by listening carefully to the words in the prompts, which contain words from the text.

**T** **Life Story of a Butterfly**

By Charlotte Guillain, published by Heinemann-Raintree

**What Is a Butterfly?**

**P1** A butterfly is a type of animal called an insect. Insects are animals with three pairs of legs and a body with three main parts. Many insects have wings. There are many types of butterflies. They live in many places around the world and can be different sizes and colors.

**Title:** Highlight the title.

**A Butterfly's Life Story**

**P2** Like all other animals, a butterfly goes through different stages as it grows into an adult. These stages make up an animal's life story. Follow the life story of butterflies, and watch them change in unusual ways as they develop and grow.

**Paragraph 2:** Highlight what the author wants you to follow.

**It Starts with an Egg**

**P3** A butterfly starts its life as an egg. The egg is oval shaped, tiny, and white. A butterfly's mother usually lays one egg under a leaf. A sticky substance holds the egg onto the plant.

**Heading for Paragraph 3:** Highlight the word that tells you something is beginning.

**Paragraph 3:** Highlight the words the author uses to describe the egg.

**The Egg Hatches**

**P4** After three to five days, the larva starts to hatch from the egg. A butterfly larva is usually called a caterpillar. This tiny caterpillar is pale, with a dark head to start with. As it grows it changes color.

**Paragraph 4:** Highlight the signal word the author uses to tell you what's next.

**Paragraph 4:** Highlight the words the author uses to describe the caterpillar.

**A Growing Caterpillar**

**P5** The caterpillar starts to eat. First it eats its own egg, and then it starts to feed on the plants around it. It gets bigger and bigger. The caterpillar grows so much that its skin splits several times. When its skin splits, the caterpillar crawls out with a soft new skin.

**Paragraph 5:** Highlight the sequence signal words.

**Paragraph 5:** Highlight the verb, or action word, that tells you how the caterpillar gets out of its old skin.

— CONTINUED

# LESSON 2: Life Story of a Butterfly, Grades 2–3
## DAY 2: Teacher-led Highlight Prompts

### Changing into a Pupa

**P6** When a caterpillar is very fat, it cannot grow any bigger. It makes a sticky liquid and attaches itself to a twig or leaf. The caterpillar's skin splits one more time. A pupa is now underneath. The pupa has a hard shell. A pupa is sometimes called a chrysalis. The stage when a caterpillar changes into an adult is called a pupa. This change of body shape is called metamorphosis. It takes a monarch butterfly about 10 days to turn into an adult. Other butterflies can take months to change into adults.

### Changing into an Adult

**P7** When a pupa has changed into an adult butterfly, the shell around it splits open. It slowly comes out of the shell. The adult butterfly's wings are soft and damp at first. It has to wait a few hours for its wings to dry and its body to get harder. Like all insects, an adult butterfly has three body parts. These are the head, the thorax, and the abdomen. On a butterfly's head there are two eyes and two antennae, which it uses to smell food. In its mouth is a long tube called a proboscis, which it uses to suck up food.

### Mating

**P8** The butterfly looks for a mate, so they can continue the life story. Together they can reproduce and create new butterflies.

**Paragraph 6:** Highlight what the caterpillars skin does again.

**Paragraph 6:** Highlight what is hard.

**Heading for Paragraph 7:** Highlight the heading above paragraph 7.

**Paragraph 7:** Highlight what the butterfly's wings are.

**Paragraph 8:** Highlight why the butterfly looks for a mate.

## Question 2 Discussion: How does the text say it?

After highlighting the text for Question 2, discuss with students what they highlighted. Be sure to point out that what they have highlighted helps to identify the text structure of the text as well as author's craft. When you begin this discussion, you will need to provide scaffolding until students are able to identify these elements independently. Below are the elements to discuss with students to answer Question 2: How does the text say it?

## Text Structure

Say: *This is a sequence text structure. What signal words did we highlight to show that the text is a sequence piece?* (after, first, then, one more time)

## Author's Craft

Say: *The author uses headings, verbs, and adjectives to convey the message about the life story of a butterfly. Why did she use headings in this text?* (Answers may include: The author used headings to help show the sequence of the stages to becoming a butterfly. Headings also tell the main idea for the section of text.) As students move to independence, they can respond on the Respond to Reading page to Q2: How does the text say it? (See Appendix, p. 140.)

# LESSON 2: Life Story of a Butterfly, Grades 2–3
## DAY 3: Q3: What does the text mean?—Interpret Text/Critical Thinking

CCSS.ELA-LITERACY.CCRA.R.8

Review all the guided highlights from Questions 1 and 2, and consider the meaning of the text through discussion. Guide students to interpret the text by considering the meaning of the text. This discussion may need to be scaffolded, depending on student ability.

Say: *The message of the text is that butterflies go through different stages as they grow into adults.*

Guide a discussion with students to help them understand the author's purpose in writing this text. You will also help them to make an inference about the author's perspective.

Say: *The author's purpose in writing this text is to tell the life story of a butterfly. Why do you think the author wants you to know about the life story of a butterfly?* (Answers will vary but may include: It is important to know how living things change and to better understand our environment.)

As students move to independence, they can respond on the Respond to Reading page to Q3: What does the text mean? (See Appendix, p. 141.)

## DAY 3: Q4: What does it mean to my life?—Applications and Connections

CCSS.ELA-LITERACY.CCRA.R.9

Guide students in making connections. By making connections, students are able to have a deeper understanding of what they read.

**Text-to-text:** Ask students to relate this text to other passages or books about life cycles. If necessary, show text that has been previously read about life cycles, and ask students to identify similarities and/or differences.

**Text-to-self:** Discuss the following question with students. You can have them turn and talk with a partner or share as a group.

• *What stages of a butterfly's life cycle have you seen?*

**Text-to-world:** Discuss the following question with students. You can have them turn and talk with a partner or share as a group.

• *How is the process described in this text similar to what happens to other living things in the world?* (Living things change as they get older.)

As students move to independence, they can respond on the Respond to Reading page to Q4: What does it mean to my life? (See Appendix, p. 141.)

## Extended Thinking Activities to Apply and Synthesize Text

- Have students complete the Life Story of a Butterfly Sequence Graphic Organizer on page 111.

- Purchase caterpillars, and have students keep a journal about the changes the caterpillar goes through.

- Read other books about life cycles and do a comparison.

## Writing Extensions

- You may choose to complete the Life Story of a Butterfly Sequence Graphic Organizer from the Extended Thinking Activities. Then have students use this to assist in completing the Sequencing Paragraph Frame on page 135.

- You can explicitly teach students to write an expository sequence text using the Sequencing Paragraph Frame. Model and scaffold the paragraph frame with students until they move to independence.

- Encourage students to apply the text structure to an explanation of another life cycle, with a diagram, using text evidence from research.

# LESSONS FOR DESCRIPTION TEXT STRUCTURE

CCSS.ELA-LITERACY.CCRA.R.1, CCSS.ELA-LITERACY.CCRA.R.2, CCSS.ELA-LITERACY.CCRA.R.3

Build the context for the reading by activating prior knowledge using the following:

## Background Knowledge

Say: *Beetles are insects that have a shell-like exterior and their bodies are tough. Most beetles have two pairs of wings. The first pair is small and hard and also protects the second pair of wings. A ladybug is a type of beetle. Beetles can be found on land and in fresh water all over the world. Most beetles live for about one year.*

## Anticipatory Set

Before you start the session, go to YouTube and search "Top 5 Unusual Facts About Ladybugs." Enlarge the video to the size of your screen, and watch it with students. Use the discussion stems below to have a brief conversation with the students about the video.

### Video Discussion

- What kind of insect is a ladybug?
  (Small spotted beetle)

- What do ladybugs do during the winter months?
  (Hibernate)

- How are ladybugs helpful in the world around us?
  (They eat garden pests.)

## Vocabulary

Explicitly teach the vocabulary words from the text. Use one or more of the suggested activities, which are meant to be direct and brief:

- Give a student-friendly definition of the word using an online dictionary as a resource. We have provided this definition.

- Add words to a visual word bank that can be created in the front of the class, on an easel, or on chart paper.

- Chant or cheer the words three to five times, pronouncing them accurately each time.

- Give students an oral example of how the word is used and relate it to something they already know.

  **antennae:** parts of an insect that help it feel
  **crawling:** moving with one's body close to the ground; this also describes how a beetle moves
  **larvae:** baby beetles
  **wings:** parts of an insect that help it fly

## Directions for Teacher-guided Prompts for Highlighting Text

1. Prior to Day 1, create an enlarged copy of the text so you can model how to highlight specific information. Depending on student ability, students can either interact with the enlarged text (using the tools referenced on page 15) or, if appropriate, their own copies of the text. Choose one color to highlight responses to the prompts.

2. Read the text out loud. Students can choral/echo read the text based on their instructional needs.

3. Before reading the prompts, explain to students that the first day of reading the text and highlighting the key ideas and details will lead to a summary of the text.

4. Either read the text in its entirety and then read the GHR prompts, or read the text line by line. Guide students to find the words to highlight by listening carefully to the words in the prompts, which contain words from the text.

## Beetles

By Rebecca Rissman, published by Heinemann-Raintree

L1 Do you see that insect crawling on the ground?

L2 It's a shiny beetle! Look at what we've found.

L3 What about this green beetle? Can you see it over there?

L4 Its wings are strong and shiny, to keep it in the air.

L5 Are all beetles the same color? What colors have you seen?

L6 Some are black, or red, or blue, and some are even green!

L7 Look at this black beetle. It's swimming in a puddle.

L8 Can you see its trail of tiny floating bubbles!

L9 Beetles can be different, but some things are always true.

L10 Beetles have six legs. And antennae? They have two.

L11 How many body parts do beetles have? How many can you see?

L12 Let's count them together: 1, 2, 3!

L13 Where can you find beetles? Look up, down, here, and there.

L14 Beetles are clever bugs. They can live almost anywhere.

L15 Baby beetles, called larvae, don't look like their dad or mom.

L16 But beetles look more like their parents the older they become.

L17 What do beetles eat, when they're crawling through the weeds?

L18 They eat other bugs and plants, and sometimes even seeds!

**Line 1:** Highlight what is crawling on the ground.

**Line 2:** Highlight the insect that is crawling on the ground.

**Line 14:** Highlight where beetles live.

**Line 15:** Highlight what baby beetles are called.

**Line 18:** Highlight what beetles eat, besides seeds.

## Question 1 Discussion and Summary: What does the text say?

Encourage students to turn and talk with a partner about what they highlighted and why they think these are the key ideas or important pieces of information in the text. Then display the words below on a board or on chart paper. Ask students to review the words and use them to complete the sentence frame summary. Guide and scaffold students with this activity as needed.

### Summary Word Bank

**beetle, insect**

This informational text describes a kind of _____ called a _____ .
(This informational text describes a kind of insect called a beetle.)

CCSS.ELA-LITERACY.CCRA.R.4, CCSS.ELA-LITERACY.CCRA.R.5, CCSS.ELA-LITERACY.CCRA.R.6

## Review Summary from Day 1

Revisit the summaries the students generated on Day 1.

## Anticipatory Set

Re-engage students on Day 2 with a second viewing of the video. After viewing the video, use the sentence frame to have students turn and talk with a partner and share one thing they learned from the video.

## Video Discussion

In the video about _____ , I learned _____ .

## Vocabulary Day 2

In order to scaffold the text for all students, vocabulary is revisited and a more in-depth analysis of the words is conducted. You can choose from one or more of the following activities to reinforce and expand vocabulary development.

- Create a visual presentation using the vocabulary terms.
- Present words in a graphic organizer, such as a Frayer Model.
- Make a headline for one of the vocabulary words as if it were a newspaper or an online article.
- Use one vocabulary word to create shades of meaning cards.
- Use the word in a metaphor with students, or have them come up with their own metaphors.

- For more specific vocabulary instruction, refer to Marzano's Six-Step Process for Vocabulary Instruction: providing a description, giving an explanation or example of the new term, restating the definition in the student's own words, creating a picture, engaging in specific activities and discussing the terms with other students in class, and involving the words in games so students can play with the terms.

**antennae:** parts of an insect that help it feel

**crawling:** moving with one's body close to the ground; this also describes how a beetle moves

**larvae:** baby beetles

**wings:** parts of an insect that help it fly

## Teacher-led Summary for Q2: How does the text say it?

This is a teacher-led summary that can be removed as students become more independent in identifying the text structure, author's craft, and text features.

Say: *This is an informational text with a description text structure. The passage includes descriptive language,* *such as color words, to describe what beetles look like and action words to describe how beetles behave. The author describes beetles in a way that helps you picture what they look like.*

## Directions for Teacher-guided Prompts for Highlighting Text

1. Use a different color to highlight the text on Day 2. Use the same highlighting method as Day 1.

2. Before reading the prompts to students, explain that the second read is to answer Q2: How does the text say it? This time they'll look at the text for a deeper meaning and discuss how the author wrote the text. You will want to point out to students that authors are purposeful when they write.

3. Either read the text in its entirety and then read the prompts for highlighting, or read the text line by line and have students highlight the text after each line is read aloud.

4. Read prompts for students to highlight the answers in the text. Guide students to find the word(s) in the text to highlight.

**T Beetles**

By Rebecca Rissman, published by Heinemann-Raintree

**L1** Do you see that insect crawling on the ground?

**L2** It's a shiny beetle! Look at what we've found.

**L3** What about this green beetle? Can you see it over there?

**L4** Its wings are strong and shiny, to keep it in the air.

**L5** Are all beetles the same color? What colors have you seen?

**L6** Some are black, or red, or blue, and some are even green!

**L7** Look at this black beetle. It's swimming in a puddle.

**L8** Can you see its trail of tiny floating bubbles!

**L9** Beetles can be different, but some things are always true.

**L10** Beetles have six legs. And antennae? They have two.

**L11** How many body parts do beetles have? How many can you see?

**L12** Let's count them together: 1, 2, 3!

**L13** Where can you find beetles? Look up, down, here, and there.

**L14** Beetles are clever bugs. They can live almost anywhere.

**L15** Baby beetles, called larvae, don't look like their dad or mom.

**L16** But beetles look more like their parents the older they become.

**L17** What do beetles eat, when they're crawling through the weeds?

**L18** They eat other bugs and plants, and sometimes even seeds!

**Title:** Highlight the title of the text.

**Line 1:** Highlight the question mark at the end.

**Line 2:** Highlight the exclamation point the author uses to show expression.

**Line 4:** Highlight the adjectives the author uses to describe the wings.

**Line 6:** Highlight the three commas the author uses to separate the different colors of beetles.

**Line 7:** Highlight the adjective that describes the color of the beetle.

**Line 9:** Highlight what beetles can be.

**Line 10:** Highlight the number word that tells how many legs beetles have.

**Line 10:** Highlight the number word that tells how many antennae beetles have.

**Line 13:** Highlight the three punctuation marks that separate the different places to look.

**Line 14:** Highlight the word that describes what beetles are.

**Line 15:** Highlight what baby beetles don't look like.

**Line 16:** Highlight what beetles look more like when they become older.

**Line 17:** Highlight the verb the author uses to show how beetles move though the weeds.

**On any two lines:** Highlight the two words that rhyme, or sound alike. (Answers may include: weeds, seeds.)

## Question 2 Discussion: How does the text say it?

After highlighting the text for Question 2, discuss what they highlighted. Explain that it helps identify text structure and author's craft. When you begin this discussion, provide scaffolding until students are able to identify these elements independently. Below are the elements to discuss with students to answer Question 2: How does the text say it?

## Text Structure

Say: *How do we know this is a description text structure?* (The author describes how beetles look and act.)

## Author's Craft

Say: *The author uses rhyme. Why do you think she chose to write in rhyme?* (So it's more fun to read.)

Say: *The author describes beetles using adjectives. Which adjectives did we highlight?*
(Answers may include: strong, shiny, black, different, and clever.)

# LESSON 3: Beetles, Grades K–1
## DAY 3: Q3: What does the text mean?—Interpret Text/Critical Thinking

CCSS.ELA-LITERACY.CCRA.R.8

Review all the guided highlights from Questions 1 and 2, and consider the meaning of the text through discussion. Guide students to interpret the text by considering the meaning of the text. This discussion may need to be scaffolded, depending on student ability.

Say: *The message of this text is that even though there are many different kinds of beetles, they still have many things in common. They all have six legs, three body parts, and two antennae.*

Guide a discussion with students to understand the author's purpose in writing this text. You will also guide them to make an inference to determine some important details that the author left out. Through collaborative conversation, students may have varied interpretations of the author's purpose for writing the text.

Say: *In lines 15 and 16, the author says that baby beetles don't look like their dad or mom. Then she says that older beetles look more like their parents. The passage doesn't say it, but there must be some type of change that happens for the beetle to look like its parents when it's older. I made an inference to figure this out. What types of changes have to happen for the larvae to look more like beetles?* (Answers may include: They have to go through the life cycle, which would include changing from larvae into small beetles. Then from small beetles, or baby beetles, they would change into adult beetles.)

Say: *The author's purpose for writing this text is to describe beetles and how they act. Why do you think the author wants us to know this information?* (Answers will vary but may include: To understand what beetles look like.)

## DAY 3: Q4: What does it mean to my life?—Applications and Connections

CCSS.ELA-LITERACY.CCRA.R.9

Guide students in making connections. By making connections, students are able to have a deeper understanding of what they read.

**Text-to-text:** Ask students to relate this text to other passages or books about beetles. If necessary, show text that has been previously read about beetles and/or insects, and ask students to identify similarities and/or differences.

**Text-to-self:** Discuss the following questions with students. You can have them turn and talk with a partner or share as a group.

• *Have you ever seen a beetle in its natural habitat? What was it doing? What did it look like?* (Answers may vary.)

**Text-to-world:** Discuss the following question with students. You can have them turn and talk with a partner or share as a group.

• *How are beetles helpful in our environment?* (Answers may include: In the video it says that beetles eat garden pests, so they help plants and garden plants stay healthy.)

## Extended Thinking Activities to Apply and Synthesize Text

- Have students complete the Beetles Description Graphic Organizer on page 114 using descriptive words from the text.

- Have students draw a diagram of a beetle and label the wings, legs, and antennae.

- Have students compare a beetle to another insect they are familiar with, such as an ant. You can discuss this in a whole group or in partners.

## Writing Extensions

- You may choose to complete the Beetles Description Graphic Organizer from the Extended Thinking Activities. Then have students use this to assist in completing the Description Paragraph Frame on page 136.

- You can explicitly teach students to write a description text using the Description Paragraph Frame. Model and scaffold the paragraph frame with students until the gradual release of responsibility moves to independence.

- Encourage students to select something from the text to draw a picture of and use text evidence to write a sentence about their pictures.

CCSS.ELA-LITERACY.CCRA.R.1, CCSS.ELA-LITERACY.CCRA.R.2, CCSS.ELA-LITERACY.CCRA.R.3

Build the context for the reading by activating prior knowledge using the following:

## Background Knowledge

Say: *Sharks are fascinating fish. There are more than 400 different species of sharks living in the oceans today. Every ocean on Earth contains sharks. Sharks have powerful teeth and jaws and are very fast swimmers.*

## Anticipatory Set

Before you start the session, go to YouTube and search for "Aqua Kids Shark Encounter." Enlarge the video to the size of your screen, and watch it with students. Use the discussion stems below to have a brief conversation with the students about the video.

### Video Discussion

- How do sharks search for food in the water? (They sense the vibration that prey make in the water.)

- Is the Caribbean reef shark an aggressive species? (No)

## Vocabulary

Explicitly teach the vocabulary words from the text. Use one or more of the suggested activities, which are meant to be direct and brief:

- Give a student-friendly definition of the word using an online dictionary as a resource. We have provided this definition.

- Add words to a visual word bank that can be created in the front of the class, on an easel, or on chart paper.

- Chant or cheer the words three to five times, pronouncing them accurately each time.

- Give students an oral example of how the word is actually used and relate it to something they already know.

> **attack:** go after prey
> **cartilage:** the strong, bendable material that makes up some parts of the body in humans and other animals
> **denticles:** tiny scales that cover a shark's skin
> **flexible:** easy to bend or move around
> **prey:** an animal hunted by another animal for food

## Directions for Teacher-guided Prompts for Highlighting Text

1. Prior to Day 1, photocopy the text passage from the Appendix for each student. Work with students in a whole-group setting with one enlarged copy of the displayed text so you can model how to highlight specific information. Students will choose one color to highlight their responses to the prompts.

2. Read the text out loud. Students can choral/echo read the text based on their instructional needs.

3. Before reading the prompts, explain to students that the first day of reading the text and highlighting the key ideas and details will lead to a summary of the text.

4. Either read the text in its entirety and then read the GHR prompts, or read the text line by line. Guide students to find the words to highlight by listening carefully to the words in the prompts, which contain words from the text.

## Sharks

By Megan Cooley Peterson, published by Capstone

**Teeth and Jaws**

**P1** Chomp! Sharks have sharp teeth and strong jaws. They use them to catch **prey**.

**P2** When sharks **attack**, their jaws pull away from the skull. A shark is able to open its mouth very wide to bite prey.

**P3** When a shark's tooth wears out, a new tooth moves in to replace it. Some sharks go through as many as 30,000 teeth in their lifetime.

**P4** Horn sharks crush the shells of shellfish with their flat back teeth.

**Speedy Swimmers**

**P5** Swoosh! Sharks move their heads from side to side when they swim. Sharks can't swim backward.

**P6** A shark's skeleton is made of **cartilage** instead of bone. Flexible cartilage makes swimming easier. Your nose and ears are also made of cartilage.

**Skin and Scales**

**P7** Tiny scales called **denticles** cover a shark's skin. Denticles look like small teeth. They make a shark's skin feel like sandpaper.

**P8** Denticles come in many shapes and sizes. They act like armor to protect sharks. Water flows smoothly over denticles, which help sharks swim fast.

**Paragraph 1:** Highlight two things the author says that sharks have.

**Paragraph 2:** Highlight what pulls away from the shark's skull when it attacks.

**Paragraph 2:** Highlight what is able to open its mouth very wide.

**Paragraph 2:** Highlight what a shark bites.

**Paragraph 3:** Highlight what can wear out.

**Paragraph 5:** Highlight what sharks do when they swim.

**Paragraph 6:** Highlight what makes swimming easier for the shark.

**Paragraph 8:** Highlight what denticles help a shark do fast.

— CONTINUED

## Question 1 Discussion and Summary: What does the text say?

Encourage students to turn and talk with a partner about what they highlighted and why they think these are the key ideas or important pieces of information in the text. Create a word bank on chart paper or displayed on a whiteboard using words below to guide students to a summary. Scaffold students with this activity as needed.

As students move to independence, they can write a summary under Q1: What does the text say? on the Respond to Reading page. (See Appendix, p. 140.)

### Summary Word Bank

jaws, prey, shark, swim, teeth

# LESSON 4: Sharks, Grades 2–3
## DAY 2: Q2: How does the text say it?—Close Read

CCSS.ELA-LITERACY.CCRA.R.4, CCSS.ELA-LITERACY.CCRA.R.5, CCSS.ELA-LITERACY.CCRA.R.6

## Review Summary from Day 1

Revisit the summaries the students generated on Day 1.

## Anticipatory Set

Re-engage students on Day 2 with a second viewing of the video. Use the discussion stem below to have a brief conversation with the students about the video.

### Video Discussion

In the video about _____ , I learned _____ .

## Vocabulary Day 2

In order to scaffold the text for all students, vocabulary is revisited and a more in-depth analysis of the words is conducted. You can choose from one or more of the following activities to reinforce and expand vocabulary development.

• Create a visual presentation using the vocabulary terms.

• Present words in a graphic organizer, such as a Frayer Model.

• Make a headline for one of the vocabulary words as if it were a newspaper or an online article.

• Use one vocabulary word to create shades of meaning cards.

• Use the word in a metaphor with students, or have them come up with their own metaphors.

• For more specific vocabulary instruction, Refer to Marzano's Six-Step Process for Vocabulary Instruction: providing a description, giving an explanation or example of the new term, restating the definition in the student's own words, creating a picture, engaging in specific activities and discussing the terms with other students in class, and involving the words in games so students can play with the terms.

**attack:** go after prey

**cartilage:** the strong, bendable material that makes up some parts of the body in humans and other animals

**denticles:** tiny scales that cover a shark's skin

**flexible:** easy to bend or move around

**prey:** an animal hunted by another animal for food

## Teacher-led Summary for Q2: How does the text say it?

This is a teacher-led summary that can be removed as students become more independent in identifying the text structure, author's craft, and text features.

Say: *This informational article has a text structure that describes sharks to readers. The passage uses descriptive words, such as "flexible" and "smoothly." The text even uses a simile to describe how a "shark's skin feels like sandpaper."*

## Directions for Teacher-guided Prompts for Highlighting Text

1. Read the text out loud.

2. Choose a different color highlighter for Day 2.

3. Before reading the prompts to students, explain that the second read is to answer Q2: How does the text say it? They will look at the text through a different lens. This time they'll look at the text for a deeper meaning and discuss how the author wrote the text. Explain that authors intentionally use words and author's craft to convey their message and purpose for the text.

4. Either read the text in its entirety and then read the prompts for highlighting, or read the text line by line. Guide students to find the words to highlight by listening carefully to the words in the prompts, which contain words from the text.

T
# Sharks

By Megan Cooley Peterson, published by Capstone

**Teeth and Jaws**

P1 Chomp! Sharks have sharp teeth and strong jaws. They use them to catch prey.

P2 When sharks attack, their jaws pull away from the skull. A shark is able to open its mouth very wide to bite prey.

P3 When a shark's tooth wears out, a new tooth moves in to replace it. Some sharks go through as many as 30,000 teeth in their lifetime.

P4 Horn sharks crush the shells of shellfish with their flat back teeth.

**Speedy Swimmers**

P5 Swoosh! Sharks move their heads from side to side when they swim. Sharks can't swim backward.

P6 A shark's skeleton is made of cartilage instead of bone. Flexible cartilage makes swimming easier. Your nose and ears are also made of cartilage.

**Skin and Scales**

P7 Tiny scales called denticles cover a shark's skin. Denticles look like small teeth. They make a shark's skin feel like sandpaper.

P8 Denticles come in many shapes and sizes. They act like armor to protect sharks. Water flows smoothly over denticles, which help sharks swim fast.

**Title:** Highlight the title.

**Heading:** Highlight the heading above paragraph 1.

**Paragraph 1:** Highlight the onomatopoeia, or sound word, used in the lead.

**Paragraph 1:** Highlight the punctuation mark that shows excitement.

**Paragraph 1:** Highlight the two adjectives in the second sentence.

**Paragraph 2:** Highlight the action word, or verb, that describes what a shark does with its prey.

**Paragraph 3:** Highlight the number used that tells us how many teeth sharks can go through in their lifetime.

**Paragraph 4:** Highlight the action word, or verb, in the sentence.

**Paragraph 4:** Highlight the descriptive word the author uses to tell what kind of back teeth the horn shark has in its mouth.

**Heading for Paragraph 5:** Highlight the heading above paragraph 5.

**Paragraph 5:** Highlight the onomatopoeia, or sound word, used in the lead.

**Paragraph 6:** Highlight what human body parts are also made of cartilage.

**Paragraph 7:** Highlight what denticles are.

**Paragraph 7:** Highlight the simile used to describe a shark's skin.

**Paragraph 8:** Highlight the simile that describes the denticles.

**All paragraphs:** Highlight how the author identifies important vocabulary words that are defined throughout the text.

— CONTINUED

## Question 2 Discussion: How does the text say it?

After highlighting the text for Question 2, discuss with students what they highlighted. Be sure to point out to students that what they have highlighted helps to identify the text structure of the text as well as author's craft. When you begin this discussion, you will need to provide scaffolding until students are able to identify these elements independently.

Below are the elements to discuss with students to answer Question 2: How does the text say it?

## Text Structure

Say: *How do we know this is a description text structure?* (The author uses describing words to tell us what the shark looks like, how it moves, and what it feels like.) *What describing words did we highlight to show that this text is a descriptive piece?* (chomp, sharp, strong, speedy, crush) *What similes did the author use to describe the shark's appearance?* (a shark's skin feels like sandpaper; They act like armor to protect shark.)

## Author's Craft

Say: *The author uses action words, or verbs, to demonstrate how the different types of sharks use their teeth and jaws. Why do you think the author used words like "chomp" to tell how the teeth and jaws move?* (Answers may include: To help you visualize how sharks bite their prey.) As students move to independence, they can respond on the Respond to Reading page to Q2: How does the text say it? (See Appendix, p. 140.)

# LESSON 4: Sharks, Grades 2–3
## DAY 3: Q3: What does the text mean?—Interpret Text/Critical Thinking

CCSS.ELA-LITERACY.CCRA.R.8

Review all the guided highlights from Questions 1 and 2, and consider the meaning of the text through discussion. Guide the students to interpret the text by considering the meaning of the text. This discussion may need to be scaffolded, depending on student ability.

Say: *The message of the text is that sharks are strong ocean creature that use their unique physical features to catch their prey.*

Guide a discussion with students to help them understand the author's purpose in writing this text. Also guide students to make an inference to better understand the author's purpose.

Say: *Why do you think the author wants you to know about sharks and their unique appearance?* (The author wants us to know that the characteristics of a shark, such as their teeth, jaw, swimming ability, skin, and scales, give it the ability to adapt and survive in its habitat.)

As students move to independence, they can respond on the Respond to Reading page to Q3: What does the text mean? (See Appendix, p. 141.)

## DAY 3: Q4: What does it mean to my life?—Applications and Connections

CCSS.ELA-LITERACY.CCRA.R.9

Guide students in making connections. By making connections, students are able to have a deeper understanding of what they read.

**Text-to-text:** Ask students to relate this text to other passages or books about sharks. If necessary, show text that has been previously read about sharks, and ask students to identify similarities and/or differences.

**Text-to-self:** Discuss the following questions with students. You can have them turn and talk with a partner or share as a group.

• *Our nose and ears are made of cartilage like a shark's skeleton. Move your nose and ears and feel the cartilage. What do you think a shark's skeleton is like?* (Answers will vary but may include: A shark's skeleton is flexible or bendable.)

• *How do you think cartilage helps sharks move under water?* (Answers will vary but may include: It helps the shark move its tail from side to side and move its body from side to side, which helps it swim faster.)

**Text-to-world:** Discuss the following question with students. You can have them turn and talk with a partner or share as a group.

• *People are scared of sharks. Why do you think that is?* (Answers will vary but may include: People are scared of sharks because they have such strong jaws and teeth that help them catch their prey very easily. People are scared that they may be mistaken for prey.)

As students move to independence, they can respond on the Respond to Reading page to Q4: What does it mean to my life? (See Appendix, p. 141.)

## Extended Thinking Activities to Apply and Synthesize Text

- Have students complete the Sharks Description Graphic Organizer on page 117 using descriptive words from the text.

- Have students draw a diagram of a shark and label the teeth, jaw, and denticles.

## Writing Extensions

- You may choose to complete the Sharks Description Graphic Organizer from the Extended Thinking Activities. Then have students use this to help them complete the Description Paragraph Frame on page 136.

- You can explicitly teach students to write an expository description text using the Description Paragraph Frame. Model and scaffold the paragraph frame with students until they move to independence.

- Encourage student groups to apply the text structure to a shared research project on a specific type of shark as a class, and then write a descriptive piece using that information.

# LESSONS FOR COMPARE/ CONTRAST TEXT STRUCTURE

CCSS.ELA-LITERACY.CCRA.R.1, CCSS.ELA-LITERACY.CCRA.R.2, CCSS.ELA-LITERACY.CCRA.R.3

## Background Knowledge

Say: *A moth and a butterfly are similar, or alike, but there are differences that can help you figure out which is which. One difference is that a butterfly is more colorful than a moth. Also, a moth has a thicker body than a butterfly.*

## Anticipatory Set

Before you start the session, go to YouTube and search for "Difference Between Moth & Butterfly." Enlarge the video to the size of your screen, and watch it with students. Read the captions as the video is played. Use the discussion stems below to have a brief conversation with the students about the video.

## Video Discussion

- What do a moth's antennae look like? (Feathery)

- According to the video, a moth is active at night. When is a butterfly active? (During the day)

- According to the pictures in the video, which is more colorful: a moth or a butterfly? (Butterfly)

## Vocabulary

Explicitly teach the vocabulary words from the text. Use one or more of the suggested activities, which are meant to be direct and brief:

- Give a student-friendly definition of the word using an online dictionary as a resource. We have provided this definition.

- Add words to a visual word bank that can be created in the front of the class, on an easel, or on chart paper.

- Chant or cheer the words three to five times, pronouncing them accurately each time.

- Give students an oral example of how the word is used and relate it to something they already know.

> **chrysalis:** hard casing that protects a butterfly as it turns into an adult
>
> **cocoon:** covering made from silk that protects a caterpillar while it grows into a moth
>
> **nocturnal:** active at night
>
> **transformation:** big change in something

## Directions for Teacher-guided Prompts for Highlighting Text

1. Prior to Day 1, create an enlarged copy of the text so you can model how to highlight specific information. Depending on student ability, students can either interact with the enlarged text (using the tools referenced on page 15) or, if appropriate, their own copies of the text. Choose one color to highlight responses to the prompts.

2. Read the text out loud. Students can choral/echo read the text based on their instructional needs.

3. Before reading the prompts, explain to students that the first day of reading the text and highlighting the key ideas and details will lead to a summary of the text.

4. Either read the text in its entirety and then read the GHR prompts, or read the text line by line. Guide students to find the words to highlight by listening carefully to the words in the prompts, which contain words from the text.

## What Is It? Moth or Butterfly?

By Jill Erfourth, Theresa Hasenauer, and Lorri Zieleniewski

**P1** Suppose a beautiful insect lands on your arm while you are outside. You see six legs and two antennae, and it has wings. You know it's either a moth or a butterfly. But which is it? Butterflies and moths have a lot in common. They both have 6 legs. They both have wings. They also start out the same way, as caterpillars. A butterfly and a moth both go through a big transformation before becoming flying adults!

**P2** So what makes them different? First of all, moths are **nocturnal,** or come out at night. On the other hand, butterflies come out during the day. Moths are also different in that they form a cocoon around themselves, and butterflies form a chrysalis around themselves.

**P3** Butterflies are usually more colorful than moths and have a thin, smooth body. Moths are different because they have thick, fuzzy bodies. Their antennae differ as well. The antennae on a butterfly are long and wider at the end, while a moth's antennae are thin and like a feather.

**P4** These differences are sure to make it easier to decide whether an insect is a moth or a butterfly!

**Paragraph 1:** Highlight what two things have a lot in common.

**Paragraph 1:** Highlight what they both start out as.

**Paragraph 1:** Highlight what they both go through before becoming adults.

**Paragraph 2:** Highlight what are nocturnal.

**Paragraph 2:** Highlight when butterflies come out.

**Paragraph 2:** Highlight what moths form around themselves.

**Paragraph 2:** Highlight what butterflies form around themselves.

**Paragraph 3:** Highlight what is colorful and has a thin, smooth body.

**Paragraph 3:** Highlight what has a thick, fuzzy body.

**Paragraph 3:** Highlight what a moth and a butterfly are.

## Question 1 Discussion and Summary: What does the text say?

Encourage students to turn and talk with a partner about what they highlighted and why they think these are the key ideas or important pieces of information in the text. Then display the words below on a board or on chart paper. Ask students to review the words and use them to complete the sentence frame summary. Guide and scaffold students with this activity as needed.

### Summary Word Bank

**butterflies, insect, moths, transformation**

_____ and _____ are both a type of _____
that goes through a _____ .
(Moths and butterflies are both a type of insect that goes through a transformation.)

CCSS.ELA-LITERACY.CCRA.R.4, CCSS.ELA-LITERACY.CCRA.R.5, CCSS.ELA-LITERACY.CCRA.R.6

## Review Summary from Day 1

Revisit the summaries the students generated on Day 1.

## Anticipatory Set

Re-engage students on Day 2 with a second viewing of the video. After viewing the video, use the sentence frame to have students turn and talk with a partner and share one thing they learned from the video.

### Video Discussion

In the video about _____, I learned _____ .

## Vocabulary Day 2

In order to scaffold the text for all students, vocabulary is revisited and a more in-depth analysis of the words is conducted. You can choose from one or more of the following activities to reinforce and expand vocabulary development.

- Create a visual presentation using the vocabulary terms.
- Present words in a graphic organizer, such as a Frayer Model.
- Make a headline for one of the vocabulary words as if it were a newspaper or an online article.
- Use one vocabulary word to create shades of meaning cards.
- Use the word in a metaphor with students, or have them come up with their own metaphors.

- For more specific vocabulary instruction, refer to Marzano's Six-Step Process for Vocabulary Instruction: providing a description, giving an explanation or example of the new term, restating the definition in the student's own words, creating a picture, engaging in specific activities and discussing the terms with other students in class, and involving the words in games so students can play with the terms.

**chrysalis:** hard casing that protects a butterfly as it turns into an adult

**cocoon:** covering made from silk that protects a caterpillar while it grows into a moth

**nocturnal:** active at night

**transformation:** big change in something

## Teacher-led Summary for Q2: How does the text say it?

This is a teacher-led summary that can be removed as students become more independent in identifying the text structure, author's craft, and text features.

Say: *This article has a text structure that compares and contrasts moths and butterflies. The authors use the signals words "common," "both," "different," and "on the other hand," and each insect is described so you can visualize how they are similar and different.*

## Directions for Teacher-guided Prompts for Highlighting Text

1. Use a different color to highlight the text on Day 2. Use the same highlighting method as Day 1.

2. Before reading the prompts to students, explain that the second read is to answer Q2: How does the text say it? This time they'll look at the text for a deeper meaning and discuss how the author wrote the text. You will want to point out to students that authors are purposeful when they write.

3. Either read the text in its entirety and then read the prompts for highlighting, or read the text line by line and have students highlight the text after each line is read aloud.

4. Read prompts for students to highlight the answers in the text. Guide students to find the word(s) in the text to highlight.

**T** ## What Is It? Moth or Butterfly?

By Jill Erfourth, Theresa Hasenauer, and Lorri Zieleniewski

**P1** Suppose a beautiful insect lands on your arm while you are outside. You see six legs and two antennae, and it has wings. You know it's either a moth or a butterfly. But which is it? Butterflies and moths have a lot in common. They both have 6 legs. They both have wings. They also start out the same way, as caterpillars. A butterfly and a moth both go through a big transformation before becoming flying adults!

**P2** So what makes them different? First of all, moths are **nocturnal**, or come out at night. On the other hand, butterflies come out during the day. Moths are also different in that they form a cocoon around themselves, and butterflies form a chrysalis around themselves.

**P3** Butterflies are usually more colorful than moths and have a thin, smooth body. Moths are different because they have thick, fuzzy bodies. Their antennae differ as well. The antennae on a butterfly are long and wider at the end, while a moth's antennae are thin and like a feather.

**P4** These differences are sure to make it easier to decide whether an insect is a moth or a butterfly!

**Title:** Highlight the title and the punctuation in the title.

**Paragraph 1:** Highlight what butterflies and moths have.

**Paragraph 1:** Highlight the first signal word used to compare moths and butterflies.

**Paragraph 1:** Highlight the number of legs they have.

**Paragraph 1:** Highlight the punctuation mark in the last sentence that shows excitement.

**Paragraph 2:** Highlight the first sentence, which is a question.

**Paragraph 2:** Highlight the word in bold print that the authors define in the text.

**Paragraph 2:** Highlight the signal phrase that lets you know this is a compare and contrast text.

**Paragraph 3:** Highlight the two words the author uses to describe the butterfly's body.

**Paragraph 3:** Highlight the two words the author uses to describe the moth's body.

**Paragraph 3:** Highlight the two words that describe the butterfly's antennae.

**Paragraph 3:** Highlight the word that describes a moth's antennae.

**Paragraph 3:** Highlight the words the author uses to describe what a moth's antennae is like.

**Paragraph 4:** Highlight the punctuation mark the author uses to show expression in the last sentence.

## Question 2 Discussion: How does the text say it?

After highlighting the text for Question 2, discuss with students the techniques of craft and structure the authors use in the text, which is what students have highlighted. When you begin this discussion, you will need to provide scaffolding until students are able to identify these elements independently.

## Text Structure

Say: *Which highlighted words signal the two insects being compared?* (common, both, on the other hand, different)

## Author's Craft

Say: *The authors use adjectives to describe the moth's and butterfly's bodies. Discuss how these word choices help you visualize the two insects. (Discuss the use of voice with the exclamation point in paragraph 4 as possible.)*

# LESSON 5: What Is It? Moth or Butterfly?, Grades K–1
## DAY 3: Q3: What does the text mean?—Interpret Text/Critical Thinking

CCSS.ELA-LITERACY.CCRA.R.8

Review all the guided highlights from Questions 1 and 2, and consider the meaning of the text through discussion. Guide students to interpret the text by considering the meaning of the text. This discussion may need to be scaffolded, depending on student ability.

Say: *The message of this text is that moths and butterflies are unique because of their differences, even though they have similar parts.*

Guide a discussion with students to understand the authors' purpose in writing this text. Through collaborative conversation, students may have varied interpretations of the authors' purpose for writing the text. Leading questions, such as the following, will guide students to possible interpretations.

Say: *Why do you think the authors want you to know how moths and butterflies are different?* Allow time for students to respond. *The authors may want us to know that even though moths and butterflies might look alike, they are different. They go through big changes in order to become adults. The authors may also assume many people do not know the difference between a moth and a butterfly, but after reading the text, the reader will be sure to know the difference.*

## DAY 3: Q4: What does it mean to my life?—Applications and Connections

CCSS.ELA-LITERACY.CCRA.R.9

Guide students in making connections. By making connections, students are able to have a deeper understanding of what they read.

**Text-to-text:** Ask students to relate this text to other passages or books about butterflies and/or moths. If necessary, show text that has been previously read about butterflies and moths, and ask students to identify similarities and/or differences.

**Text-to-self:** Discuss the following questions with students. You can have them turn and talk with a partner or share as a group.

• *Have you ever seen a moth or a butterfly? Moths and butterflies go through stages in life in order to become adults. What other stages of life have you seen in your environment?* (Answers will vary but may include: Trees, plants, pets such as dogs and cats.)

**Text-to-world:** Discuss the following question with students. You can have them turn and talk with a partner or share as a group.

• *The wings on moths and butterflies are very fragile and shouldn't be touched so they won't be damaged. What would you say to someone entering a butterfly home or environment?* (You would tell them to be very careful not to touch a butterfly's wings.)

## LESSON 5: What Is It? Moth or Butterfly?, Grades K–1
DAY 4:

## Extended Thinking Activities to Apply and Synthesize Text

- Have students complete the What Is It? Moth or Butterfly? Venn Diagram on page 119 using information from the text.

- Model how to find more information on butterflies and moths.

- Order caterpillars online, and let students see the transformation. Keep a picture log of the changes the caterpillar goes through.

- Have students create their own illustrations of butterflies and moths with art supplies by following the descriptions in the passage.

## Writing Extensions

- You may choose to complete the What Is It? Moth or Butterfly? Venn Diagram from the Extended Thinking Activities. Then have students use this to assist in completing the Compare/Contrast Paragraph Frame on page 137.

- You can explicitly teach students to write an expository compare/contrast text using the Compare/Contrast Paragraph Frame. Model and scaffold the paragraph frame with students until they move to independence.

- Encourage students to write a descriptive sentence for each insect, using evidence from the text.

CCSS.ELA-LITERACY.CCRA.R.1, CCSS.ELA-LITERACY.CCRA.R.2, CCSS.ELA-LITERACY.CCRA.R.3

Build the context for the reading by activating prior knowledge using the following:

## Background Knowledge

Say: *Some children go to school throughout the year but have longer breaks during the school year. Some children don't attend school in the summer but have shorter breaks during the year.*

## Anticipatory Set

Before you start the session, go to YouTube and search for "Year Round School Plans" by WLOS News 13. Enlarge the video to the size of your screen, and watch it with students. Use the discussion stems below to have a brief conversation with the students about the video.

## Video Discussion

- What will be increased over time by year-round school? (Student achievement)

- How do the parents who attended it as students themselves feel about year-round school? (They liked it.)

## Vocabulary

Explicitly teach the vocabulary words below from the text. Use one or more of the suggested activities, which are meant to be direct and brief:

- Give a student-friendly definition of the word using an online dictionary as a resource. We have provided this definition.

- Add words to a visual word bank that can be created in the front of the class, on an easel, or on chart paper.

- Chant or cheer the words three to five times, pronouncing them accurately each time.

- Give students an oral example of how the word is used and relate it to something they already know.

**contrast:** comparison of what is different
**traditional:** what people are used to doing

## Directions for Teacher-guided Prompts for Highlighting Text

1. Prior to Day 1, photocopy the text passage from the Appendix for each student. Work with students in a whole-group setting with one enlarged copy of the displayed text so you can model how to highlight specific information. Students will choose one color to highlight their responses to the prompts.

2. Read the text out loud. Students can choral/echo read the text based on their instructional needs.

3. Before reading the prompts, explain to students that the first day of reading the text and highlighting the key ideas and details will lead to a summary of the text.

4. Either read the text in its entirety and then read the GHR prompts, or read the text line by line. Guide students to find the words to highlight by listening carefully to the words in the prompts, which contain words from the text.

## Year-round School or Traditional School?

By Jill Erfourth, Theresa Hasenauer, and Lorri Zieleniewski

**P1** Wait...I thought there was no school in July or August! We have to go to school in the summer? Schools across the country are switching their traditional nine-month calendars to a year-round calendar for many reasons. While both schedules provide children a great learning opportunity, they have their educational differences.

**Paragraph 1:** Highlight what schools across the country are switching their nine-month calendars to.

**P2 Year-round School**

A year-round calendar does not have an extended summer vacation but rather shorter breaks throughout the year. Students get to enjoy time off in every season. It has benefits to students, such as avoiding the "summer slide" upon returning to school. They won't forget material they've learned. Also, the lazy days of summer eventually get pretty boring, so going to school actually gives kids something to do.

**Paragraph 2:** Highlight what a year-round calendar has instead of an extended summer vacation.

**Paragraph 2:** Highlight what the children won't forget if they attend school in the summer.

**P3 Traditional Nine-month Calendar**

In **contrast,** the traditional school year was designed around a nine-month school year with almost three months off in the summer. But did you know that the original purpose of the traditional school calendar with extended summer vacation was to allow children to harvest the crops on the farms? This is hardly the case now. However, if children go to school in the summer, then they have less time to play in the warm weather and less time to splash around in pools. Instead of attending action-packed summer camps where kids can explore their talents and interests, children would be attending school to continue their learning. Year-round school could put a damper on vacation plans for many families who often plan trips during the summer months.

**Paragraph 3:** Highlight what is designed around a nine-month school year with three months off in the summer.

**Paragraph 3:** Highlight the original purpose of the traditional school calendar.

**Paragraph 3:** Highlight what a year-round school could put a damper on.

**P4** Both school calendars have a great deal to offer students! After carefully comparing the advantages and disadvantages, would you like to go to school all year-round?

— CONTINUED

## Question 1 Discussion and Summary: What does the text say?

Encourage students to turn and talk with a partner about what they highlighted and why they think these are the key ideas or important pieces of information in the text. Create a word bank on chart paper or displayed on a whiteboard using words below to guide students to a summary. Scaffold students with this activity as needed.

As students move to independence, they can write a summary under Q1: What does the text say? on the Respond to Reading page. (See Appendix, p. 140.)

### Summary Word Bank

**school, traditional, year-round**

CCSS.ELA-LITERACY.CCRA.R.4, CCSS.ELA-LITERACY.CCRA.R.5, CCSS.ELA-LITERACY.CCRA.R.6

## Review Summary from Day 1

Revisit the summaries the students generated on Day 1.

## Anticipatory Set

Re-engage students on Day 2 with a second viewing of the video. After viewing the video, use the sentence frame to have students turn and talk with a partner and share one thing they learned from the video.

### Video Discussion

In the video about _____ , I learned _____ .

## Vocabulary Day 2

In order to scaffold the text for all students, vocabulary is revisited and a more in-depth analysis of the words is conducted. You can choose from one or more of the following activities to reinforce and expand vocabulary development.

• Create a visual presentation using the vocabulary terms.

• Present words in a graphic organizer, such as a Frayer Model.

• Make a headline for one of the vocabulary words as if it were a newspaper or an online article.

• Use one vocabulary word to create shades of meaning cards.

• Use the word in a metaphor with students, or have them come up with their own metaphors.

• For more specific vocabulary instruction, Refer to Marzano's Six-Step Process for Vocabulary Instruction: providing a description, giving an explanation or example of the new term, restating the definition in the student's own words, creating a picture, engaging in specific activities and discussing the terms with other students in class, and involving the words in games so students can play with the terms.

**contrast:** comparison of what is different
**traditional:** what people are used to doing

## Teacher-led Summary for Q2: How does the text say it?

This is a teacher-led summary that can be removed as students become more independent in identifying the text structure, author's craft, and text features.

Say: *In this compare/contrast text structure, the authors state that there are advantages and disadvantages to going to school all year-round. The authors use signal words, such as "in contrast," "however," and "both," to help the reader understand this text structure.*

## Directions for Teacher-guided Prompts for Highlighting Text

1. Read the text out loud.

2. Choose a different color highlighter for Day 2.

3. Before reading the prompts to students, explain that the second read is to answer Q2: How does the text say it? They will look at the text through a different lens. This time they'll look at the text for a deeper meaning and discuss how the author wrote the text. Explain that authors intentionally use words and author's craft to convey their message and purpose for the text.

4. Either read the text in its entirety and then read the prompts for highlighting, or read the text line by line. Guide students to find the words to highlight by listening carefully to the words in the prompts, which contain words from the text.

**T** ## Year-round School or Traditional School?

By Jill Erfourth, Theresa Hasenauer, and Lorri Zieleniewski

**P1** Wait...I thought there was no school in July or August! We have to go to school in the summer? Schools across the country are switching their traditional nine-month calendars to a year-round calendar for many reasons. While both schedules provide children a great learning opportunity, they have their educational differences.

**P2** ### Year-round School

A year-round calendar does not have an extended summer vacation but rather shorter breaks throughout the year. Students get to enjoy time off in every season. It has benefits to students, such as avoiding the "summer slide" upon returning to school. They won't forget material they've learned. Also, the lazy days of summer eventually get pretty boring, so going to school actually gives kids something to do.

**P3** ### Traditional Nine-month Calendar

In contrast, the traditional school year was designed around a nine-month school year with almost three months off in the summer. But did you know that the original purpose of the traditional school calendar with extended summer vacation was to allow children to harvest the crops on the farms? This is hardly the case now. However, if children go to school in the summer, then they have less time to play in the warm weather and less time to splash around in pools. Instead of attending action-packed summer camps where kids can explore their talents and interests, children would be attending school to continue their learning. Year-round school could put a damper on vacation plans for many families who often plan trips during the summer months.

**P4** Both school calendars have a great deal to offer students! After carefully comparing the advantages and disadvantages, would you like to go to school all year-round?

**Title:** Highlight the title.

**Paragraph 1:** Highlight the catchy introduction that shows the authors' voice.

**Paragraph 1:** Highlight the punctuation mark showing a question.

**Heading for Paragraph 2:** Highlight the heading above paragraph 2.

**Paragraph 2:** Highlight the catchy phrase the authors use that's in quotation marks.

**Paragraph 2:** Highlight the adjective used to describe summer days.

**Heading for Paragraph 3:** Highlight the heading above paragraph 3.

**Paragraph 3:** Highlight the first set of signal words that shows this is a compare/contrast text structure.

**Paragraph 3:** Highlight the next signal word in the paragraph that shows that the text is a compare/contrast.

**Paragraph 3:** Highlight the third set of signal words that shows this is a compare/contrast text structure.

**Paragraph 4:** Highlight the signal words that show this is a compare/contrast text structure.

**Paragraph 4:** Highlight the question the authors are asking the audience.

— CONTINUED

## Question 2 Discussion: How does the text say it?

After highlighting the text for Question 2, discuss with students what they highlighted. Be sure to point out to students that what they have highlighted helps to identify the text structure of the text as well as author's craft. When you begin this discussion, you will need to provide scaffolding until students are able to identify these elements independently.

Below are the elements to discuss with students to answer Question 2: How does the text say it?

## Text Structure

Say: *This text compares and contrasts going to school year-round and attending school with summers off. What signal words did we highlight to show that this text is a compare/contrast piece?* (in contrast, however, instead of, both)

## Author's Craft

Say: *The authors use a creative lead to grab the reader's attention. How did the authors' choice of words help you understand the text?* (Answers may include: It helps describe how a student might feel if he or she had to go to school year-round.) *Why do you think the author asks the reader questions throughout the text?* (Answers may include: It helps the reader think about the text while reading and make connections.)

As gradual release of responsibility moves to independence, students can respond on the Respond to Reading page to Q2: How does the text say it? (See Appendix, p. 140.)

# LESSON 6: Year-round School or Traditional School?, Grades 2–3
## DAY 3: Q3: What does the text mean?—Interpret Text/Critical Thinking

CCSS.ELA-LITERACY.CCRA.R.8

Review all the guided highlights from Questions 1 and 2, and consider the meaning of the text through discussion. Guide the students to interpret the text by considering the meaning of the text. This discussion may need to be scaffolded, depending on student ability.

Say: *The message of this text is that the year-round school calendar has advantages and disadvantages just like the traditional school calendar.*

Guide a discussion with students to understand the authors' purpose in writing this text.

Say: *The authors' purpose in this text is to compare the calendar of year-round school to the traditional school calendar. Why do you think the authors wanted to share this information with readers?* (The authors wanted us to know that the calendars are different and that there are advantages and disadvantages to both calendars. They also wanted us to think about which type of school year we'd prefer.)

As gradual release of responsibility moves to independence, students can respond on the Respond to Reading page to Q3: What does the text mean? See Appendix, p. 141.)

## DAY 3: Q4: What does it mean to my life?—Applications and Connections

CCSS.ELA-LITERACY.CCRA.R.9

Guide students in making connections. By making connections, students are able to have a deeper understanding of what they read.

**Text-to-text:** Ask students to relate this text to other passages or books about year-round school and traditional school. If possible, show text that has been previously read about year-round school and traditional school, and ask students to identify similarities and/or differences.

**Text-to-self:** Discuss the following questions with students. You can have them turn and talk with a partner or share as a group.

• *Would you prefer to attend year-round school or traditional school?*

• *Why do you feel this way?*

• *In what type of school do you think you would learn the most and be the happiest?*

**Text-to-world:** Discuss the following question with students. You can have them turn and talk with a partner or share as a group.

• *Since children no longer stay home to help their parents harvest crops like they did many years ago, do you think all schools should change to a year-round calendar?*

As students move to independence, they can respond on the Respond to Reading page to Q4: What does it mean to my life? (See Appendix, p. 141.)

## Extended Thinking Activities to Apply and Synthesize Text

- Have students complete the Year-round School or Traditional School? Venn Diagram on page 122.

- Have students take a stand on which type of school year they prefer and why. Have them list two reasons for their opinions.

## Writing Extensions

- You may choose to complete the Year-round School or Traditional School? Venn Diagram from the Extended Thinking Activities. Then have students use this to assist in completing the Compare/Contrast Paragraph Frame on page 137.

- You can explicitly teach students to write an expository compare/contrast text using the Compare/Contrast Paragraph Frame. Model and scaffold the paragraph frame with students until they move to independence.

- Encourage student groups to apply the text structure to a debate for or against year-round school. Have students use evidence from the text and other sources to back up their reasons.

# LESSONS FOR CAUSE/EFFECT TEXT STRUCTURE

CCSS.ELA-LITERACY.CCRA.R.1, CCSS.ELA-LITERACY.CCRA.R.2, CCSS.ELA-LITERACY.CCRA.R.3

Build the context for the reading by activating prior knowledge using the following:

## Background Knowledge

Say: *Germs on our hands can really get us sick. They are so small, we cannot see them and don't know they are in our body until we get sick. They can be easily spread too. When we touch our eyes, mouths, or noses with our hands and then touch other things around us, we can get other people sick. Just the same, if you have touched things with germs on them and then touch your eyes, nose, or mouth, you can get sick. The best way to stop the spread of germs is to wash your hands.*

## Anticipatory Set

Before you start the session, go to YouTube and search for "The Hand Wash Song by Krazy Kuzins." Enlarge the video to the size of your screen, and watch it with students. Use the discussion stems below to have a brief conversation with the students about the video.

## Video Discussion

- Name two steps that you do when washing your hands. (Answers may include: turn on water, scrub with soap.)

- Why should we wash our hands? (To keep germs away)

## Vocabulary

Explicitly teach the vocabulary words from the text. Use one or more of the suggested activities, which are meant to be direct and brief:

- Give a student-friendly definition of the word using an online dictionary as a resource. We have provided this definition.

- Add words to a visual word bank that can be created in the front of the class, on an easel, or on chart paper.

- Chant or cheer the words three to five times, pronouncing them accurately each time.

- Give students an oral example of how the word is used and relate it to something they already know.

**germs:** tiny organisms that can make us sick and can spread

**horrible:** very bad

**intruders:** things that come in without being asked

## Directions for Teacher-guided Prompts for Highlighting Text

1. Prior to Day 1, create an enlarged copy of the text so you can model how to highlight specific information. Depending on student ability, students can either interact with the enlarged text (using the tools referenced on page 15) or, if appropriate, their own copies of the text. Choose one color to highlight responses to the prompts.

2. Read the text out loud. Students can choral/echo read the text based on their instructional needs.

3. Before reading the prompts, explain to students that the first day of reading the text and highlighting the key ideas and details will lead to a summary of the text.

4. Either read the text in its entirety and then read the GHR prompts, or read the text line by line. Guide students to find the words to highlight by listening carefully to the words in the prompts, which contain words from the text.

## Wash Those Germs Away!

By Jill Erfourth, Theresa Hasenauer, and Lorri Zieleniewski

**L1** Our bodies are awesome!

**L2** Did you know pesky intruders try to get in our bodies and make us sick?

**L3** Those intruders are called germs.

**L4** Washing your hands is one of the best ways to stop the spread of germs.

**L5** Germs like to snuggle inside your body and cause you to get sick.

**L6** Blah!

**L7** If you don't wash your hands a lot, then you can pick up germs that can enter your body and make you feel horrible.

**L8** By rubbing your eyes, nose or mouth with germy hands that haven't been washed, you can make yourself and your whole family sick!

**L9** So if you see friends sneezing or coughing into their hands, remind them to go wash their hands!

**L10** You don't want to get sick, do you?

**Line 1:** Highlight what is awesome.

**Line 2:** Highlight what tries to get into our bodies and make us sick.

**Line 3:** Highlight what the intruders are called?

**Line 5:** Highlight what germs cause you to get.

**Line 7:** Highlight what you could pick up if you do not wash your hands a lot.

**Line 9:** Highlight what you should remind your friends to do when they are sneezing or coughing.

## Question 1 Discussion and Summary: What does the text say?

Encourage students to turn and talk with a partner about what they highlighted and why they think these are the key ideas or important pieces of information in the text. Then display the words below on a board or on chart paper. Ask students to review the words and use them to complete the sentence frame summary. Guide and scaffold students with this activity as needed.

### Summary Word Bank

**germs, sick**

Not washing your hands can cause you to pick up _____ . The effects of _____ is that you can get _____ , which makes you sneeze, cough, and feel horrible.

(Not washing your hands can cause you to pick up germs. The effect of germs is that you can get sick, which makes you sneeze, cough, and feel horrible.)

# LESSON 7: Wash Those Germs Away!, Grades K–1
## DAY 2: Q2: How does the text say it?—Close Read

CCSS.ELA-LITERACY.CCRA.R.4, CCSS.ELA-LITERACY.CCRA.R.5, CCSS.ELA-LITERACY.CCRA.R.6

## Review Summary from Day 1

Revisit the summaries the students generated on Day 1.

## Anticipatory Set

Re-engage students on Day 2 with a second viewing of the video. After viewing the video, use the sentence frame to have students turn and talk with a partner and share one thing they learned from the video.

## Video Discussion

In the video about _____ , I learned _____ .

## Vocabulary Day 2

In order to scaffold the text for all students, vocabulary is revisited and a more in-depth analysis of the words is conducted. You can choose from one or more of the following activities to reinforce and expand vocabulary development.

• Create a visual presentation using the vocabulary terms.

• Present words in a graphic organizer, such as a Frayer Model.

• Make a headline for one of the vocabulary words as if it were a newspaper or an online article.

• Use one vocabulary word to create shades of meaning cards.

• Use the word in a metaphor with students, or have them come up with their own metaphors.

• For more specific vocabulary instruction, refer to Marzano's Six-Step Process for Vocabulary Instruction: providing a description, giving an explanation or example of the new term, restating the definition in the student's own words, creating a picture, engaging in specific activities and discussing the terms with other students in class, and involving the words in games so students can play with the terms.

**germs:** tiny organisms that can make us sick and can spread

**horrible:** very bad

**intruders:** things that come in without being asked

## Teacher-led Summary for Q2: How does the text say it?

This is a teacher-led summary that can be removed as students become more independent in identifying the text structure, author's craft, and text features.

Say: *This informational text tells you the cause (not washing hands) and the effect it can have on you (you can get germs that make you sick). The cause tells you why something happened and the effect is what happened. Signal words, like "if" and "then" or "so" and "by," let you know this is a cause/effect text.*

## Directions for Teacher-guided Prompts for Highlighting Text

1. Use a different color to highlight the text on Day 2. Use the same highlighting method as Day 1.

2. Before reading the prompts to students, explain that the second read is to answer Q2: How does the text say it? This time they'll look at the text for a deeper meaning and discuss how the author wrote the text. You will want to point out to students that authors are purposeful when they write.

3. Either read the text in its entirety and then read the prompts for highlighting, or read the text line by line and have students highlight the text after each line is read aloud.

4. Read prompts for students to highlight the answers in the text. Guide students to find the word(s) in the text to highlight.

**T   Wash Those Germs Away!**

By Jill Erfourth, Theresa Hasenauer, and Lorri Zieleniewski

**L1**  Our bodies are awesome!

**L2**  Did you know pesky intruders try to get in our bodies and make us sick?

**L3**  Those intruders are called germs.

**L4**  Washing your hands is one of the best ways to stop the spread of germs.

**L5**  Germs like to snuggle inside your body and cause you to get sick.

**L6**  Blah!

**L7**  If you don't wash your hands a lot, then you can pick up germs that can enter your body and make you feel horrible.

**L8**  By rubbing your eyes, nose or mouth with germy hands that haven't been washed, you can make yourself and your whole family sick!

**L9**  So if you see friends sneezing or coughing into their hands, remind them to go wash their hands!

**L10**  You don't want to get sick, do you?

**Title:** Highlight the title.

**Line 1:** Highlight the exclamation point that shows the authors' excitement.

**Line 2:** Highlight the adjective used to describe the intruders.

**Line 3:** Highlight the period that shows the end of the sentence.

**Line 6:** Highlight the sound word.

**Line 7:** Highlight the two signal words that show this is a cause/effect text.

**Line 7:** Highlight the comma.

**Line 8:** Highlight the first word in the sentence, which is a signal word to show a cause/effect relationship.

**Line 8:** Highlight what will make you and your whole family sick.

**Line 9:** Highlight the first word in the sentence, which is another signal word that shows cause/effect.

**Line 10:** Highlight the punctuation mark that shows this is a question.

## Question 2 Discussion: How does the text say it?

After highlighting the text for Question 2, discuss with students the techniques of craft and structure the authors use in the text, which is what students have highlighted. When you begin this discussion, you will need to provide scaffolding until students are able to identify these elements independently. Below are the elements to discuss with students to answer Question 2: How does the text say it?

### Text Structure

Say: *The text structure is cause and effect. What signal words did we highlight to show there is a cause/effect text structure?* (if, then, by, so)

### Author's Craft

Say: *What sound word did the authors use?* (Blah) *The authors use many types of punctuation marks to get their message across. What types of punctuation marks did the authors use?* (Commas, periods, question marks, and exclamation points) *Why did the authors use an exclamation point in sentences 1, 6, 8, and 9?* (Answers may include: The authors used the exclamation points there to show expression, or to say those words with excitement.)

# LESSON 7: Wash Those Germs Away!, Grades K–1
## DAY 3: Q3: What does the text mean?—Interpret Text/Critical Thinking

CCSS.ELA-LITERACY.CCRA.R.8

Review all the guided highlights from Questions 1 and 2, and consider the meaning of the text through discussion. Guide students to interpret the text by considering the meaning of the text. This discussion may need to be scaffolded, depending on student ability.

Say: *The message of this text is that it's important to wash your hands so that you don't spread germs and get sick.*

Guide a discussion with students to understand the authors' purpose in writing this text. Support students as they make an inference from the text to determine the authors' purpose. Through collaborative conversation, students may have varied interpretations.

Say: *Why do you think the authors want you to know that germs can make you sick?* (Answers may include: Being sick can make other people sick.) Say: *The authors may want us to know that simply washing our hands can keep us from spreading germs and getting ourselves and others sick. What parts of the text lead us to understanding this? Look at lines 4 and 7.* (Washing your hands is one of the best ways to stop the spread of germs; If you don't wash your hands a lot, then you can pick up germs that can enter your body and make you feel horrible.)

## DAY 3: Q4: What does it mean to my life?—Applications and Connections

CCSS.ELA-LITERACY.CCRA.R.9

Guide students in making connections. By making connections, students are able to have a deeper understanding of what they read.

**Text-to-text:** Ask students to relate this text to other passages or books about getting sick. If necessary, show text that has been previously read about germs, and ask students to identify similarities and/or differences.

**Text-to-self:** Discuss the following questions with students. You can have them turn and talk with a partner or share as a group.

• *Have you ever been sick? What did your body feel like when you were sick?* (Answers may include: achy, cold, hot, miserable.)

• *What would have prevented the illness?* (Answers may include: washing hands.)

**Text-to-world:** Discuss the following questions with students. You can have them turn and talk with a partner or share as a group.

• *Why is it important for everyone to wash their hands?* (So people do not spread germs to other people.)

• *What can we do at school to prevent spreading germs?* (Wash our hands after using the restroom, before eating snack or lunch, etc.)

• *Winter is a time of year when people get sick. What can we do to keep everyone healthy? Use evidence from the text.* (In the text, the authors say we should remind our friends to wash their hands. Another thing we can do to stay healthy is cover our mouths when we cough.)

## Extended Thinking Activities to Apply and Synthesize Text

- Have students complete the Wash Those Germs Away! Cause/Effect Graphic Organizer on page 125.

- Discuss the proper way to wash hands and the suggested length of time using the alphabet song. Encourage students to come up with other songs that they can wash their hands to.

- Have students draw or list when they should wash their hands to prevent spreading germs and getting sick.

## Writing Extensions

- You may choose to complete the Wash Those Germs Away! Cause/Effect Graphic Organizer from the Extended Thinking Activities. Then have students use this to assist in completing the Cause/Effect Paragraph Frame on page 138.

- You can explicitly teach students to write an expository cause/effect text using the Cause/Effect Paragraph Frame. Model and scaffold the paragraph frame with students until they move to independence.

- Encourage students to use the cause/effect text structure to write about a time when they were sick with a cold or flu. Younger students can draw pictures and add captions.

CCSS.ELA-LITERACY.CCRA.R.1, CCSS.ELA-LITERACY.CCRA.R.2, CCSS.ELA-LITERACY.CCRA.R.3

Build the context for the reading by activating prior knowledge using the following:

## Background Knowledge

Say: *Taking care of our Earth includes thinking about the carbon footprint we leave behind. Our carbon footprint measures how much we change Earth by using its fossil fuels for energy. Fossil fuels include coal, oil, and natural gas. When we burn these fossil fuels, they release harmful gases into the atmosphere, or air.*

## Anticipatory Set

Before you start the session, go to YouTube and search for "Schoolhouse Rock: Earth Don't Be a Carbon Sasquatch." Enlarge the video to the size of your screen, and watch it with students. Use the discussion stems below to have a brief conversation with the students about the video.

### Video Discussion

- What are carbon footprints made out of? ($CO_2$ or carbon dioxide)
- What are some things you can do to reduce your carbon footprint? (Answers may include: turn off your computer when you're not using it, walk instead of drive, etc.)
- What are the three "R" words to help our Earth? (Reduce, reuse, recycle)
- What does a smaller footprint mean? (Less pollution)

## Vocabulary

Explicitly teach the vocabulary words from the text. Use one or more of the suggested activities, which are meant to be direct and brief:

- Give a student-friendly definition of the word using an online dictionary as a resource. We have provided this definition.
- Add words to a visual word bank that can be created in the front of the class, on an easel, or on chart paper.
- Chant or cheer the words three to five times, pronouncing them accurately each time.

- Give students an oral example of how the word is used and relate it to something they already know.

**carbon footprint:** a total set of gases given off by an organization, event, or product
**energy:** a source of usable power
**fossil fuel:** a natural fuel formed from the remains of plants and animals; coal, oil, and natural gas are fossil fuels
**polluted:** made dirty or unusable by waste

## Directions for Teacher-guided Prompts for Highlighting Text

1. Prior to Day 1, photocopy the text passage from the Appendix for each student. Work with students in a whole-group setting with one enlarged copy of the displayed text so you can model how to highlight specific information. Students will choose one color to highlight their responses to the prompts.

2. Read the text out loud. Students can choral/echo read the text based on their instructional needs.

3. Before reading the prompts, explain to students that the first day of reading the text and highlighting the key ideas and details will lead to a summary of the text.

4. Either read the text in its entirety and then read the GHR prompts, or read the text line by line. Guide students to find the words to highlight by listening carefully to the words in the prompts, which contain words from the text.

### Three Cheers for Trees! A Book about Our Carbon Footprint

By Angie LePetit, published by Capstone

**P1** Every step you take on a beach leaves behind a footprint. So do wet steps on a dry sidewalk or a trek through a muddy yard. Your footprints change the places that you go. But what does a carbon footprint do?

**P2** A carbon footprint doesn't look like a foot. In fact, you can't see it at all! But it is a mark you leave behind. A carbon footprint measures how much you change Earth by using its fossil fuel energy.

**Paragraph 2:** Highlight what doesn't look like a foot.

**Paragraph 2:** Highlight what a carbon footprint is.

**Paragraph 2:** Highlight what a carbon footprint measures.

**P3** Coal, oil, and natural gas are fossil fuels. They are found deep inside Earth. They have given us energy for many years. But once we use them up, they will be gone forever.

**Paragraph 3:** Highlight the three types of fossil fuels.

**Paragraph 3:** Highlight what will happen once we use up fossil fuels.

**P4** A hot, polluted planet isn't good for anyone. That's why we need to make good choices about our energy use. The smaller our carbon footprints, the healthier we keep Earth.

**P5** It takes energy to make stuff. An easy way to shrink your carbon footprint is to reuse items. Old socks can be made into puppets. Empty jelly jars make great piggy banks. By reusing items, we keep factories from making too much stuff. It keeps Earth clean too!

**Paragraph 5:** Highlight an easy way to shrink your carbon footprint.

**P6** A big part of our carbon footprint comes from driving. Cars, buses, and trucks add a lot of pollution to the air. You can keep Earth cooler and cleaner by walking or riding your bike.

**Paragraph 6:** Highlight how you can keep Earth cooler and cleaner.

**P7** Lights off! You can reduce your carbon footprint by using less electricity at home. Remember to turn off lights and TVs when they're not in use. In the summer, ask an adult if you can turn up the thermostat a few degrees. In the winter, turn it down.

**Paragraph 7:** Highlight how you can reduce your carbon footprint.

— CONTINUED

# LESSON 8: Three Cheers for Trees!, Grades 2–3
## DAY 1: Teacher-led Highlight Prompts

**P8** There is something else that can help us use less electricity. Can you guess what? TREES! In summer trees shade our homes and keep them cool. In winter trees help keep our homes warm by blocking cold winds.

**P9** Trees are also needed to clean the air. They suck up the gas that makes Earth hot. Then trees give us oxygen to breathe. When too much gas is put in the air, trees can't keep up. This is why we need to use fewer fossil fuels. One tree makes enough oxygen for two people to breathe. Let's plant more trees!

**P10** Trees preserve life. Without them Earth would overheat. And we'd have nothing to breathe! Let's be mindful of what we use and do to take care of our planet. A smaller carbon footprint means a happier home for us all.

**Paragraph 8:** Highlight what else can help us use less electricity.

**Paragraph 9:** Highlight what trees are also needed for.

**Paragraph 10:** Highlight what trees do.

**Paragraph 10:** Highlight what would overheat without trees.

## Question 1 Discussion and Summary: What does the text say?

Encourage students to turn and talk with a partner about what they highlighted and why they think these are the key ideas or important pieces of information in the text. Create a word bank on chart paper or displayed on a whiteboard using words below to guide students to a summary. Scaffold students with this activity as needed.

As students move to independence, they can write a summary under Q1: What does the text say? on the Respond to Reading page. (See Appendix, p. 140.)

**Summary Word Bank**

**carbon footprint, Earth, fossil fuel, reuse, trees**

CCSS.ELA-LITERACY.CCRA.R.4, CCSS.ELA-LITERACY.CCRA.R.5, CCSS.ELA-LITERACY.CCRA.R.6

## Review Summary from Day 1

Revisit the summaries the students generated on Day 1.

## Anticipatory Set

Re-engage students on Day 2 with a second viewing of the video. After viewing the video, use the sentence frame to have students turn and talk with a partner and share one thing they learned from the video.

## Video Discussion

In the video about _____ , I learned _____ .

## Vocabulary Day 2

In order to scaffold the text for all students, vocabulary is revisited and a more in-depth analysis of the words is conducted. You can choose from one or more of the following activities to reinforce and expand vocabulary development.

- Create a visual presentation using the vocabulary terms.
- Present words in a graphic organizer, such as a Frayer Model.
- Make a headline for one of the vocabulary words as if it were a newspaper or an online article.
- Use one vocabulary word to create shades of meaning cards.

- For more specific vocabulary instruction, Refer to Marzano's Six-Step Process for Vocabulary Instruction: providing a description, giving an explanation or example of the new term, restating the definition in the student's own words, creating a picture, engaging in specific activities and discussing the terms with other students in class, and involving the words in games so students can play with the terms.

**carbon footprint:** a total set of gases given off by an organization, event, or product

**energy:** a source of usable power

**fossil fuel:** a natural fuel formed from the remains of plants and animals; coal, oil, and natural gas are fossil fuels

**polluted:** made dirty or unusable by waste

## Teacher-led Summary for Q2: How does the text say it?

This is a teacher-led summary that can be removed as students become more independent in identifying the text structure, author's craft, and text features.

Say: *This informational article is a cause/effect structure about the carbon footprint we leave behind and what we can do to be mindful of reducing that footprint. The author explains the effects of using too much of fossil fuel energy.*

## Directions for Teacher-guided Prompts for Highlighting Text

1. Read the text out loud.
2. Choose a different color highlighter for Day 2.
3. Before reading the prompts to students, explain that the second read is to answer Q2: How does the text say it? They will look at the text through a different lens. This time they'll look at the text for a deeper meaning and discuss how the author wrote the text. Explain that

authors intentionally use words and author's craft to convey their message and purpose for the text.

4. Either read the text in its entirety and then read the prompts for highlighting, or read the text line by line. Guide students to find the words to highlight by listening carefully to the words in the prompts, which contain words from the text.

**T** **Three Cheers for Trees! A Book about Our Carbon Footprint**

By Angie LePetit, published by Capstone

**P1** Every step you take on a beach leaves behind a footprint. So do wet steps on a dry sidewalk or a trek through a muddy yard. Your footprints change the places that you go. But what does a carbon footprint do?

**P2** A carbon footprint doesn't look like a foot. In fact, you can't see it at all! But it is a mark you leave behind. A carbon footprint measures how much you change Earth by using its fossil fuel energy.

**P3** Coal, oil, and natural gas are fossil fuels. They are found deep inside Earth. They have given us energy for many years. But once we use them up, they will be gone forever.

**P4** A hot, polluted planet isn't good for anyone. That's why we need to make good choices about our energy use. The smaller our carbon footprints, the healthier we keep Earth.

**P5** It takes energy to make stuff. An easy way to shrink your carbon footprint is to reuse items. Old socks can be made into puppets. Empty jelly jars make great piggy banks. By reusing items, we keep factories from making too much stuff. It keeps Earth clean too!

**P6** A big part of our carbon footprint comes from driving. Cars, buses, and trucks add a lot of pollution to the air. You can keep Earth cooler and cleaner by walking or riding your bike.

**P7** Lights off! You can reduce your carbon footprint by using less electricity at home. Remember to turn off lights and TVs when they're not in use. In the summer, ask an adult if you can turn up the thermostat a few degrees. In the winter, turn it down.

**Title:** Point out the title as a text feature.

**Paragraph 1:** Highlight the catchy lead the author uses to begin the text.

**Paragraph 1:** Highlight the imagery the author uses in the text to help you visualize the steps.

**Paragraph 1:** Highlight the question at the end of the paragraph that grabs your attention.

**Paragraph 4:** Highlight the two adjectives, or describing words, in the beginning of the paragraph that describe the planet.

**Paragraph 4:** Highlight what the effect is of a smaller carbon footprint.

**Paragraph 5:** Highlight the effect that reusing items has on our Earth.

**Paragraph 6:** Highlight what a big part of our carbon footprint comes from.

**Paragraph 7:** Highlight the catchy lead in paragraph 7.

**Paragraph 7:** Highlight what two things you can turn off to reduce your carbon footprint at home.

— CONTINUED

P8 There is something else that can help us use less electricity. Can you guess what? TREES! In summer trees shade our homes and keep them cool. In winter trees help keep our homes warm by blocking cold winds.

P9 Trees are also needed to clean the air. They suck up the gas that makes Earth hot. Then trees give us oxygen to breathe. When too much gas is put in the air, trees can't keep up. This is why we need to use fewer fossil fuels. One tree makes enough oxygen for two people to breathe. Let's plant more trees!

P10 Trees preserve life. Without them Earth would overheat. And we'd have nothing to breathe! Let's be mindful of what we use and do to take care of our planet. A smaller carbon footprint means a happier home for us all.

**Paragraph 8:** Highlight the two effects have during the summer.

**Paragraph 9:** Highlight what the trees suck up that makes Earth hot.

**Paragraph 9:** Highlight what trees give us to breathe.

**Paragraph 9:** Highlight the cause/effect sentence in paragraph 9.

**Paragraph 10:** Highlight what we should be mindful of.

**Paragraph 10:** Highlight the final cause/effect sentence about a smaller carbon footprint.

## Question 2 Discussion: How does the text say it?

After highlighting the text for Question 2, discuss with students what they highlighted. Be sure to point out to students that what they have highlighted helps to identify the text structure of the text as well as author's craft. When you begin this discussion, you will need to provide scaffolding until students are able to identify these elements independently.

Below are the elements to discuss with students to answer Question 2: How does the text say it?

## Text Structure

Say: *This text shows a cause/effect structure. The cause is using too much fossil fuel energy and the effects are what it does to our environment. What are the effects of using too much fossil fuel energy? (Using too much fossil fuel, the cause, can have the effect of polluting our planet.)*

## Author's Craft

Say: *The author uses several cause/effect sentences to convey her message regarding the carbon footprint and what we can do about it. The author also uses imagery and catchy leads to grab readers' attention and engage them in the text.*

As students move to independence, they can respond on the Respond to Reading page to Q2: How does the text say it? (See Appendix, p. 140.)

# LESSON 8: Three Cheers for Trees!, Grades 2–3
## DAY 3: Q3: What does the text mean?—Interpret Text/Critical Thinking

CCSS.ELA-LITERACY.CCRA.R.8

Review all the guided highlights from Questions 1 and 2, and consider the meaning of the text through discussion. Guide students to interpret the text by considering the meaning of the text. This discussion may need to be scaffolded, depending on student ability.

Say: *The message of the text is that there are many ways we can reduce our carbon footprint. We can be mindful of the fossil fuel energy we use every day.*

Guide a discussion with students to understand the author's purpose in writing this text. They may be guided to make an inference from the text to determine author's purpose. Through discussion, students may have a variety of interpretations.

Say: *The author's purpose in this book is to inform readers of what they can do to be mindful of the fossil fuel energy we use so we can reduce, or minimize, the carbon footprint we leave behind. Why do you think the author wants you to know the effects of using up our fossil fuel energy?* (Answers may include: The author wants everyone to be aware of the fossil fuel energy we use so we can do our part to help protect Earth.)

As students move to independence, they can respond on the Respond to Reading page to Q3: What does the text mean? (See Appendix, p. 141.)

## DAY 3: Q4: What does it mean to my life?—Applications and Connections

CCSS.ELA-LITERACY.CCRA.R.9

Guide students in making connections. By making connections, students are able to have a deeper understanding of what they read.

**Text-to-text:** Ask students to relate this text to other passages or books about pollution. If necessary, show text that has been previously read about protecting our environment, recycling, carbon footprints, fossil fuels, etc., and ask students to identify similarities and/or differences.

**Text-to-self:** Discuss the following questions with students. You can have them turn and talk with a partner or share as a group.

• *Have you done any of the things in the text to help reduce your carbon footprint?* (Answers may include: turning off the lights in our classroom when we leave, reusing items, etc.)

• *What specific things can you do at home to reduce your carbon footprint?* (Answers may include: turning off the lights, turning off the TV when we are done watching it, etc.)

**Text-to-world:** Discuss the following questions with students. You can have them turn and talk with a partner or share as a group.

• *What might happen if people don't do their part to protect our Earth and help keep our environment clean?* (Answers may include: Our Earth might be full of waste.)

• *What effect might that have on the future?* (Answers may include: The waste could affect our breathing and water supply.)

As students move to independence, they can respond on the Respond to Reading page to Q4: What does it mean to my life? (See Appendix, p. 141.)

## Extended Thinking Activities to Apply and Synthesize Text

- Have students complete the Three Cheers for Trees! Cause/Effect Graphic Organizer on page 129.

- Have students make a list of things they can do to reduce their carbon footprint at school.

## Writing Extensions

- You may choose to complete the Three Cheers for Trees! Cause/Effect Graphic Organizer from the Extended Thinking Activities. Then have students use this to assist in completing the Cause/Effect Paragraph Frame on page 138.

- You can explicitly teach students to write an expository cause/effect text using the Cause/Effect Paragraph Frame. Model and scaffold the paragraph frame with students until the gradual release of responsibility moves to independence.

- Encourage students to use the cause/effect text structure to write about how they can conserve energy at home. For example, they can write about how turning off the lights, computer, or other items around their house can have a long-term effect (conserves energy, lowers bills).

# LESSONS FOR PROBLEM/ SOLUTION TEXT STRUCTURE

CCSS.ELA-LITERACY.CCRA.R.1, CCSS.ELA-LITERACY.CCRA.R.2, CCSS.ELA-LITERACY.CCRA.R.3

Build the context for the reading by activating prior knowledge using the following:

## Background Knowledge

Say: *Trying to solve everyday problems to make life a little easier is the reason for many inventions. A bandage, which we often call a Band-Aid, was invented almost 100 years ago when people had to make their own bandages to cover a cut.*

## Anticipatory Set

Before you start the session, go to YouTube and search for "Band-Aid History." Please note, the title that will appear is "The Truly Bloody History: A Band-Aid Love Story." The video does not contain any blood and is appropriate for children. Enlarge the video to the size of your screen, and watch it with students. Use the discussion stems below to have a brief conversation with students about the video.

### Video Discussion

• What problem did Earle Dickson's wife have when she was cooking? (She often burnt or cut herself.)

• What did Earle Dickson make each day for his wife? (Bandages)

• What did the company Johnson & Johnson produce? (The first adhesive bandage)

## Vocabulary

Explicitly teach the vocabulary words from the text. Use one or more of the suggested activities, which are meant to be direct and brief:

• Give a student-friendly definition of the word using an online dictionary as a resource. We have provided this definition.

• Add words to a visual word bank that can be created in the front of the class, on an easel, or on chart paper.

• Chant or cheer the words three to five times, pronouncing them accurately each time.

• Give students an oral example of how the word is used and relate it to something they already know.

> **bandage:** a strip of material used to cover up a wound
> **gauze:** a very thin cloth
> **invented:** made something new
> **sticky:** coated with a gluey substance

## Directions for Teacher-guided Prompts for Highlighting Text

1. Prior to Day 1, create an enlarged copy of the text so you can model how to highlight specific information. Depending on student ability, students can either interact with the enlarged text (using the tools referenced on page 15) or, if appropriate, their own copies of the text. Choose one color to highlight responses to the prompts.

2. Read the text out loud. Students can choral/echo read the text based on their instructional needs.

3. Before reading the prompts, explain to students that the first day of reading the text and highlighting the key ideas and details will lead to a summary of the text.

4. Either read the text in its entirety and then read the GHR prompts, or read the text line by line. Guide students to find the words to highlight by listening carefully to the words in the prompts, which contain words from the text.

LESSON 9 • A STICKY IDEA

# LESSON 9: A Sticky Idea, Grades K–1
## DAY 1: Teacher-led Highlight Prompts

## A Sticky Idea

**P1** Have you ever put a sticky bandage on a cut? The best-known sticky bandages are called Band-Aids. They were invented in 1920.

**P2** A man named Earle Dickson invented Band-Aids. Earle wanted to help his wife. She often cut her fingers when she cooked.

**P3** At the time, people had to make their own bandages. They cut pieces of gauze and tape. Those bandages were hard to use. Earle's idea was easy to use. Thanks, Earle!

**Paragraph 1:** Highlight what the best-known bandages are called.

**Paragraph 1:** Highlight when they were invented.

**Paragraph 2:** Highlight who invented Band-Aids.

**Paragraph 2:** Highlight what Earle Dickson did.

**Paragraph 3:** Highlight what people had to do at that time.

## Question 1 Discussion and Summary: What does the text say?

Encourage students to turn and talk with a partner about what they highlighted and why they think these are the key ideas or important pieces of information in the text. Then display the words below on a board or on chart paper. Ask students to review the words and use them to complete the sentence frame summary. Guide and scaffold students with this activity as needed.

### Summary Word Bank

**bandages, Earle Dickson, invented**

This informational text is about _____ and how _____ _____ them.

(This informational text is about bandages and how Earle Dickson invented them.)

# LESSON 9: A Sticky Idea, Grades K–1
## DAY 2: Q2: How does the text say it?—Close Read

CCSS.ELA-LITERACY.CCRA.R.4, CCSS.ELA-LITERACY.CCRA.R.5, CCSS.ELA-LITERACY.CCRA.R.6

## Review Summary from Day 1

Revisit the summaries the students generated on Day 1.

## Anticipatory Set

Re-engage students on Day 2 with a second viewing of the video. After viewing the video, use the sentence frame to have students turn and talk with a partner and share one thing they learned from the video.

### Video Discussion

In the video about _____ , I learned _____ .

## Vocabulary Day 2

In order to scaffold the text for all students, vocabulary is revisited and a more in-depth analysis of the words is conducted. You can choose from one or more of the following activities to reinforce and expand vocabulary development.

- Create a visual presentation using the vocabulary terms.
- Present words in a graphic organizer, such as a Frayer Model.
- Make a headline for one of the vocabulary words as if it were a newspaper or an online article.
- Use one vocabulary word to create shades of meaning cards.
- Use the word in a metaphor with students, or have them come up with their own metaphors.

- For more specific vocabulary instruction, refer to Marzano's Six-Step Process for Vocabulary Instruction: providing a description, giving an explanation or example of the new term, restating the definition in the student's own words, creating a picture, engaging in specific activities and discussing the terms with other students in class, and involving the words in games so students can play with the terms.

> **bandage:** a strip of material used to cover up a wound
> **gauze:** a very thin cloth
> **invented:** made something new
> **sticky:** coated with a gluey substance

## Teacher-led Summary for Q2: How does the text say it?

This is a teacher-led summary that can be removed as students become more independent in identifying the text structure, author's craft, and text features.

Say: *This is an informational text with a problem/ solution text structure. The author explains that a man named Earle Dickson invented Band-Aids to solve the problem of people having to make their own bandages.*

## Directions for Teacher-guided Prompts for Highlighting Text

1. Use a different color to highlight the text on Day 2. Use the same highlighting method as Day 1.

2. Before reading the prompts to students, explain that the second read is to answer Q2: How does the text say it? This time they'll look at the text for a deeper meaning and discuss how the author wrote the text. You will want to point out to students that authors are purposeful when they write.

3. Either read the text in its entirety and then read the prompts for highlighting, or read the text line by line and have students highlight the text after each line is read aloud.

4. Read prompts for students to highlight the answers in the text. Guide students to find the word(s) in the text to highlight.

# LESSON 9: A Sticky Idea, Grades K–1
## DAY 2: Teacher-led Highlight Prompts

**T** **A Sticky Idea**

**P1** Have you ever put a sticky bandage on a cut? The best-known sticky bandages are called Band-Aids. They were invented in 1920.

**P2** A man named Earle Dickson invented Band-Aids. Earle wanted to help his wife. She often cut her fingers when she cooked.

**P3** At the time, people had to make their own bandages. They cut pieces of gauze and tape. Those bandages were hard to use. Earle's idea was easy to use. Thanks, Earle!

**Title:** Highlight the title.

**Paragraph 1:** Highlight the question the author begins the text with.

**Paragraph 2:** Highlight what Earle wanted to do.

**Paragraph 2:** Highlight what she often did when she cooked.

**Paragraph 3:** Highlight how people had to make their own bandages.

**Paragraph 3:** Highlight what those bandages were.

**Paragraph 3:** Highlight what was easy to use.

**Paragraph 3:** Highlight the exclamation the author uses at the end.

## Question 2 Discussion: How does the text say it?

After highlighting the text for Question 2, discuss with students the techniques of craft and structure the author uses in the text, which is what they have highlighted. Be sure to point out to students that what they have highlighted helps to identify the text structure of the text as well as author's craft. When you begin this discussion, you will need to provide scaffolding until students are able to identify these elements independently.

Below are the elements to discuss with students to answer Question 2: How does the text say it?

## Text Structure

Say: *The text structure is problem/solution. Even though there are not specific signal words to show a problem, the author explains the problem in the text. What is the problem?* (Answers may include: The problem is that people had to make their own bandages.) Say: *What is the solution to the problem in the text?* (Answers may include: The solution is that Earle invents the first adhesive bandage.)

## Author's Craft

Say: *The author uses a question at the beginning of the text. The author made this choice to engage the reader and make a personal connection to the reader. Would the text be as engaging if it started with the next line?* (No)

Say: *The author uses an exclamation point to show expression at the end of the text. How do you think the author feels about the invention of the Band-Aid?* (Answers may include: The author is thankful for the invention of Band-Aids.)

# LESSON 9: A Sticky Idea, Grades K–1
## DAY 3: Q3: What does the text mean?—Interpret Text/Critical Thinking

CCSS.ELA-LITERACY.CCRA.R.8

Review all the guided highlights from Questions 1 and 2, and consider the meaning of the text through discussion. Guide students to interpret the text by considering the meaning of the text. This discussion may need to be scaffolded, depending on student ability.

Say: *The message of the text is to explain how and why Earle Dickson invented the Band-Aid.*

Guide a discussion with students to understand the author's purpose in writing this text. Help students make an inference from the text they read and what they have highlighted. Through collaborative conversation, students may have varied interpretations of the author's purpose for writing the text.

Say: *Why do you think the author wants you to know about the invention of the Band-Aid?* (Answers may include: Many things we use today were invented by trying to solve an everyday problem. Anyone can be an inventor by trying to solve some of life's everyday problems.)

## DAY 3: Q4: What does it mean to my life?—Applications and Connections

CCSS.ELA-LITERACY.CCRA.R.9

Guide students in making connections. By making connections, students are able to have a deeper understanding of what they read.

**Text-to-text:** Ask students to relate this text to other passages or books about inventions. If necessary, show text that has been previously read about inventions, and ask students to identify similarities and/or differences.

**Text-to-self:** Discuss the following question with students. You can have them turn and talk with a partner or share as a group.

• *How has the invention of the Band-Aid helped you?* (Answers may include: Band-Aids keep our cuts clean. They also make our cuts feel better.)

**Text-to-world:** Discuss the following question with students. You can have them turn and talk with a partner or share as a group.

• *Inventions help us solve everyday problems. What are some inventions that would be difficult to live without, such as the lightbulb, computer, Internet, and microwave?*

## Extended Thinking Activities to Apply and Synthesize Text

- Have students complete A Sticky Idea Problem/Solution Graphic Organizer on page 131.

- Ask students what they might invent to solve an everyday problem, such as a better way for shoelaces to stay tied.

- Ask students to consider something they could invent that would solve a problem in the classroom, such as a self-sharpening pencil. Have students share their idea for their invention with the class or in small groups and explain why it would be helpful.

## Writing Extensions

- You may choose to complete the A Sticky Idea Problem/Solution Graphic Organizer from the Extended Thinking Activities. Then have students use this to assist in completing the Problem/Solution Paragraph Frame on page 139.

- You can explicitly teach students to write a problem/solution text using the Problem/Solution Paragraph Frame. Model and scaffold the paragraph frame with students until students move to independence.

- Encourage students to use the Problem/Solution Paragraph Frame to come up with an everyday problem or a problem at school and a way to solve it. Brainstorm problems and solutions with students as needed.

CCSS.ELA-LITERACY.CCRA.R.1, CCSS.ELA-LITERACY.CCRA.R.2, CCSS.ELA-LITERACY.CCRA.R.3

Build the context for the reading by activating prior knowledge using the following:

## Background Knowledge

Say: *Think about where your water bottle goes after you're done with it. Some people throw these kinds of things away, but we can recycle plastic, paper, and glass. There are recycling centers all over the world.*

## Anticipatory Set

Before you start the session, go to YouTube and search for "Recycling: Plastic Bottle Recycling" from eHow. Enlarge the video to the size of your screen, and watch it with students. Use the discussion stems below to have a brief conversation with the students about the video.

### Video Discussion

- How long does plastic last? (Forever)

- What happens to plastic at the recycling center? (It's ground up, cleaned, turned into pellets, and made into new plastic products.)

- What should we do with our plastic bottles when we are finished with them? (Squeeze them together and put the caps back on before putting them in your recycle bin.)

## Vocabulary

Explicitly teach the vocabulary words below from the text. Use one or more of the suggested activities, which are meant to be direct and brief:

- Give a student-friendly definition of the word using an online dictionary as a resource. We have provided this definition.

- Add words to a visual word bank that can be created in the front of the class, on an easel, or on chart paper.

- Chant or cheer the words three to five times, pronouncing them accurately each time.

- Give students an oral example of how the word is used and relate it to something they already know.

> **fossil fuel:** a natural fuel formed from the remains of plants and animals; coal, oil, and natural gas are fossil fuels
>
> **landfill:** an area of land where garbage is buried or dumped
>
> **natural resource:** something in nature that people use, such as coal, trees, and oil
>
> **oil rig:** a machine that pulls oil from deep in the earth

## Directions for Teacher-guided Prompts for Highlighting Text

1. Prior to Day 1, photocopy the text passage from the Appendix for each student. Work with students in a whole-group setting with one enlarged copy of the displayed text so you can model how to highlight specific information. Students will choose one color to highlight their responses to the prompts.

2. Read the text out loud. Students can choral/echo read the text based on their instructional needs.

3. Before reading the prompts, explain to students that the first day of reading the text and highlighting the key ideas and details will lead to a summary of the text.

4. Either read the text in its entirety and then read the GHR prompts, or read the text line by line. Guide students to find the words to highlight by listening carefully to the words in the prompts, which contain words from the text.

## Trash Magic: A Book about Recycling a Plastic Bottle

By Angie LePetit, published by Capstone

**P1** Gulp! It's easy to grab a bottle of water, juice, or soda when you are thirsty. But where do all those bottles come from? And why is it so important to recycle them? Let's find out!

**Paragraph 1:** Highlight what's easy to grab.

**Paragraph 1:** Highlight what is important to do with bottles.

**P2** To make a plastic bottle, you start with oil—a dark, sticky fossil fuel. Machines called oil rigs drill for oil deep in the earth. Long, strawlike pipes suck the oil out of the ground.

**Paragraph 2:** Highlight what you start with to make a bottle.

**Paragraph 2:** Highlight what the machines are called that drill for oil.

**P3** Making plastic from oil takes a lot of work. First, the oil must be cleaned and heated. When it's really hot, chemicals are added, and the oil thickens. As it cools, the oil turns into little crumbs called raw plastic. Raw plastic doesn't look like much. That's because it needs to get heated again. The crumbs melt together, and more chemicals are added. As the new plastic cools, it becomes stretchy. Blow air into the stretchy plastic, and you have a bottle!

**Paragraph 3:** Highlight what must be done to the oil first.

**Paragraph 3:** Highlight what's added when the oil is hot.

**Paragraph 3:** Highlight what the little crumbs are called.

**Paragraph 3:** Highlight what you have after air is blown into stretchy plastic.

**P4** It takes a lot of work and natural resources to make a plastic bottle, and millions are used every day. It's too bad not all of them get recycled. Some get tossed to the roadside as litter. Others end up in the ocean. Even more are put in the garbage and dumped in landfills.

**Paragraph 4:** Highlight what it takes to make a plastic bottle.

**Paragraph 4:** Highlight what happens to plastic bottles if they are not recycled.

— CONTINUED

**P5** Here's the problem—plastic does not easily fall apart. Remember the chemicals used to make the plastic? It takes hundreds of years for them to leave the bottles. Once they do, the chemicals soak into the ground. They can get into our water, which is not safe. Drinking these chemicals makes you sick.

**Paragraph 5:** Highlight what the problem is.

**Paragraph 5:** Highlight how long it takes for chemicals to leave the bottles.

**Paragraph 5:** Highlight where the chemicals soak into.

**P6** There's another reason to recycle plastic bottles. Do you remember what dark and sticky liquid makes plastic? That's right: oil. And where does oil come from? Right again: the ground. If we use oil too fast, we could run out.

**P7** So what can you do with an empty plastic bottle? You could wash it and reuse it. Or you could recycle it. If you want to recycle the bottle, place the bottle in a recycling bin. It's that easy!

**Paragraph 7:** Highlight what three things you can do with an empty plastic bottle.

## Question 1 Discussion and Summary: What does the text say?

Encourage students to turn and talk with a partner about what they highlighted and why they think these are the key ideas or important pieces of information in the text. Create a word bank on chart paper or displayed on a whiteboard using words below to guide students to a summary. Scaffold students with this activity as needed.

As students move to independence, they can write a summary under Q1: What does the text say? on the Respond to Reading page. (See Appendix, p. 140.)

### Summary Word Bank

**bottle, natural resources, plastic, oil, recycle**

CCSS.ELA-LITERACY.CCRA.R.4, CCSS.ELA-LITERACY.CCRA.R.5, CCSS.ELA-LITERACY.CCRA.R.6

## Review Summary from Day 1

Revisit the summaries the students generated on Day 1.

## Anticipatory Set

Before you start the session, revisit the video from Day 1. Use the discussion stem below to have a brief conversation with the students about the video.

### Video Discussion

In the video about _____ , I learned _____ .

## Vocabulary Day 2

In order to scaffold the text for all students, vocabulary is revisited and a more in-depth analysis of the words is conducted. You can choose from one or more of the following activities to reinforce and expand vocabulary development.

- Create a visual presentation using the vocabulary terms.
- Present words in a graphic organizer, such as a Frayer Model.
- Make a headline for one of the vocabulary words as if it were a newspaper or an online article.
- Use one vocabulary word to create shades of meaning cards.
- For more specific vocabulary instruction, Refer to Marzano's Six-Step Process for Vocabulary Instruction:

providing a description, giving an explanation or example of the new term, restating the definition in the student's own words, creating a picture, engaging in specific activities and discussing the terms with other students in class, and involving the words in games so students can play with the terms.

> **fossil fuel:** a natural fuel formed from the remains of plants and animals; coal, oil, and natural gas are fossil fuels
>
> **landfill:** an area of land where garbage is buried or dumped
>
> **natural resource:** something in nature that people use, such as coal, trees, and oil
>
> **oil rig:** a machine that pulls oil from deep in the earth

## Teacher-led Summary for Q2: How does the text say it?

This is a teacher-led summary that can be removed as students become more independent in identifying the text structure, author's craft, and text features.

Say: *The author conveys in this problem/solution text structure that there will be a problem with our natural resources if we don't do something now. She uses the signal words "problem" and "what can you do?"*

## Directions for Teacher-guided Prompts for Highlighting Text

1. Read the text out loud.
2. Choose a different color highlighter for Day 2.
3. Before reading the prompts to students, explain that the second read is to answer Q2: How does the text say it? They will look at the text through a different lens. This time they'll look at the text for a deeper meaning and discuss how the author wrote the text. Explain that authors intentionally use words and author's craft to convey their message and purpose for the text.
4. Either read the text in its entirety and then read the prompts for highlighting, or read the text line by line. Guide students to find the words to highlight by listening carefully to the words in the prompts, which contain words from the text.

## Trash Magic: A Book about Recycling a Plastic Bottle

By Angie LePetit, published by Capstone

**P1** Gulp! It's easy to grab a bottle of water, juice, or soda when you are thirsty. But where do all those bottles come from? And why is it so important to recycle them? Let's find out!

**P2** To make a plastic bottle, you start with oil—a dark, sticky fossil fuel. Machines called oil rigs drill for oil deep in the earth. Long, strawlike pipes suck the oil out of the ground.

**P3** Making plastic from oil takes a lot of work. First, the oil must be cleaned and heated. When it's really hot, chemicals are added, and the oil thickens. As it cools, the oil turns into little crumbs called raw plastic. Raw plastic doesn't look like much. That's because it needs to get heated again. The crumbs melt together, and more chemicals are added. As the new plastic cools, it becomes stretchy. Blow air into the stretchy plastic, and you have a bottle!

**P4** It takes a lot of work and natural resources to make a plastic bottle, and millions are used every day. It's too bad not all of them get recycled. Some get tossed to the roadside as litter. Others end up in the ocean. Even more are put in the garbage and dumped in landfills.

**P5** Here's the problem—plastic does not easily fall apart. Remember the chemicals used to make the plastic? It takes hundreds of years for them to leave the bottles. Once they do, the chemicals soak into the ground. They can get into our water, which is not safe. Drinking these chemicals makes you sick.

**Title:** Highlight the title.

**Subtitle:** Highlight the subtitle.

**Paragraph 1:** Highlight the word that is imitating a sound—also called onomatopoeia.

**Paragraph 1:** Highlight the two questions the author asks.

**Paragraph 2:** Highlight the describing words, or adjectives, the author uses to describe oil.

**Paragraph 2:** Highlight what sucks the oil out of the ground.

**Paragraph 3:** Highlight what the oil turns into as it cools.

**Paragraph 3:** Highlight the word that describes what the plastic becomes.

**Paragraph 4:** Highlight how many bottles are used everyday.

**Paragraph 5:** Highlight the signal word that tells you the text structure or how the text is organized.

— CONTINUED

P6  There's another reason to recycle plastic bottles. Do you remember what dark and sticky liquid makes plastic? That's right: oil. And where does oil come from? Right again: the ground. If we use oil too fast, we could run out.

P7  So what can you do with an empty plastic bottle? You could wash it and reuse it. Or you could recycle it. If you want to recycle the bottle, place the bottle in a recycling bin. It's that easy!

**Paragraph 6:** Highlight what the problem with oil is.

**Paragraph 7:** Highlight the question the author asks to prompt a solution to the problem.

**Paragraph 7:** Highlight the cliché at the end of the paragraph. A cliché is a phrase that is used often.

## Question 2 Discussion: How does the text say it?

After highlighting the text for Question 2, discuss with students what they highlighted. Be sure to point out to students that what they have highlighted helps to identify the text structure of the text as well as author's craft. When you begin this discussion, you will need to provide scaffolding until students are able to identify these elements independently.

Below are the elements to discuss with students to answer Question 2: How does the text say it?

## Text Structure

Say: *How do we know this is a problem/solution text structure? What signal words and phrases did we highlight to show that the text is a problem/solution piece?* (problem; So what can you do with an empty plastic bottle?)

## Author's Craft

Say: *Look at what we highlighted for "How does the text say it?" Give examples of how the author uses descriptive words and phrases in the text to help paint a picture in the reader's mind.* (Answers may include: The author uses describing words like "dark," "sticky," and "stretchy.")

Say: *The author uses literary devices in the text, such as onomatopoeia and imagery. Give an example of imagery from the text and what the imagery does for the reader.* (The author compares the pipes that suck up oil to a straw. This helps the reader picture what the pipes look like and how they work.)

As students move to independence, they can respond on the Respond to Reading page to Q2: How does the text say it? (See Appendix, p. 140.)

# LESSON 10: Trash Magic, Grades 2–3
## DAY 3: Q3: What does the text mean?—Interpret Text/Critical Thinking

CCSS.ELA-LITERACY.CCRA.R.8

Review all the guided highlights from Questions 1 and 2, and consider the meaning of the text through discussion. Guide the students to interpret the text by considering the meaning of the text. This discussion may need to be scaffolded, depending on student ability.

Say: *The message of the text is that we need to recycle, not only to help our environment but to help ensure we won't eventually run out of natural resources, such as oil.*

Guide a discussion with students to understand the author's perspective in writing this text. This is where students are guided to make an inference from the text and what they have highlighted to understand the author's perspective.

Say: *The author's purpose in writing this text is to make us aware that plastic bottles are made from oil, which is a natural resource. Why does the author think this is important for us to know?* (Answers may include: The author is informing us of something we may not know about so we're aware that if we use too much of our natural resources, they may run out. The author wants to make it clear that we need to protect our natural resources and use them wisely.)

As students move to independence, they can respond on the Respond to Reading page to Q3: What does the text mean? (See Appendix, p. 141.)

## DAY 3: Q4: What does it mean to my life?—Applications and Connections

CCSS.ELA-LITERACY.CCRA.R.9

Guide students in making connections. By making connections, students are able to have a deeper understanding of what they read.

**Text-to-text:** Ask students to relate this text to other passages or books about recycling. If necessary, show text that has been previously read about recycling and protecting the environment, and ask students to identify similarities and/or differences.

**Text-to-self:** Discuss the following question with students. You can have them turn and talk with a partner or share as a group.

• *What are some things we use that can be recycled in our homes or at school?* (Answers may include: plastic, glass, cardboard, milk carton, plastic forks and spoons, newspapers, juice containers, etc.)

**Text-to-world:** Discuss the following question with students. You can have them turn and talk with a partner or share as a group.

• *What might happen if we run out of natural resources, such as oil?* (Answers may include: If we run out of oil, we will not be able to use cars or planes. We will need to find new energy sources.)

As students move to independence, they can respond on the Respond to Reading page to Q4: What does it mean to my life? (See Appendix, p. 141).

## Extended Thinking Activities to Apply and Synthesize Text

- Have students complete the Trash Magic Problem/ Solution Graphic Organizer on page 134.

- Have student pairs discuss what might happen if we use up our natural resources. Encourage each pair to share their discussion with the whole class.

- Have students discuss ways they can reduce the amount of plastic they use each day.

## Writing Extensions

- You may choose to complete the Trash Magic Problem/ Solution Graphic Organizer from the Extended Thinking Activities. Then have students use this to assist in completing the Problem/Solution Paragraph Frame on page 139.

- You can explicitly teach students to write a problem/ solution text using the Problem/Solution Paragraph Frame. Model and scaffold the paragraph frame with students until they move to independence.

- Encourage students to use the problem/solution text structure to write an argument, convincing others to recycle.

# APPENDIX

# How Plastic Is Recycled

Published by ReadWorks.org: The Solution to Reading Comprehension.

**P1** Things made of plastic can be recycled. They can be made into something new.

**P2** People put plastic into bins. Workers take the plastic to a factory. The plastic is sorted. It is washed. Then it is chopped. The pieces are dried. They are heated and they melt. Finally, they are put into water to cool.

**P3** Now the plastic is new again! It can be used to make new things.

Name: _____

# How Plastic Is Recycled
### Sequence Graphic Organizer

Draw these steps in the correct sequence, according to the text, to show how plastic is recycled.

Finally, they are put into water to cool.

Workers take the plastic to a factory.

Then it is chopped.

The pieces are dried.

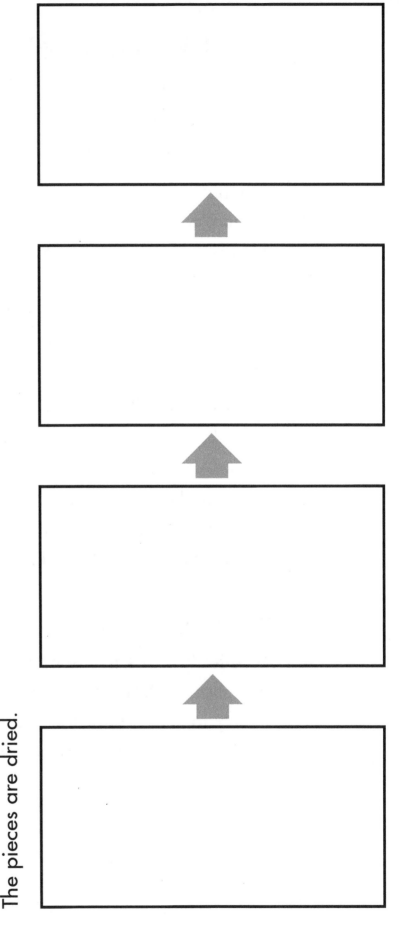

# Life Story of a Butterfly

By Charlotte Guillain, published by Heinemann-Raintree

## What Is a Butterfly?

P1 A butterfly is a type of animal called an insect. Insects are animals with three pairs of legs and a body with three main parts. Many insects have wings. There are many types of butterflies. They live in many places around the world and can be different sizes and colors.

## A Butterfly's Life Story

P2 Like all other animals, a butterfly goes through different stages as it grows into an adult. These stages make up an animal's life story. Follow the life story of butterflies, and watch them change in unusual ways as they develop and grow.

## It Starts with an Egg

P3 A butterfly starts its life as an egg. The egg is oval shaped, tiny, and white. A butterfly's mother usually lays one egg under a leaf. A sticky substance holds the egg onto the plant.

## The Egg Hatches

P4 After three to five days, the larva starts to hatch from the egg. A butterfly larva is usually called a caterpillar. This tiny caterpillar is pale, with a dark head to start with. As it grows it changes color.

## A Growing Caterpillar

P5 The caterpillar starts to eat. First it eats its own egg, and then it starts to feed on the plants around it. It gets bigger and bigger. The caterpillar grows so much that its skin splits several times. When its skin splits, the caterpillar crawls out with a soft new skin.

## Changing into a Pupa

P6 When a caterpillar is very fat, it cannot grow any bigger. It makes a sticky liquid and attaches itself to a twig or leaf. The caterpillar's skin splits one more time. A pupa is now underneath. The pupa has a hard shell. A pupa is sometimes called a chrysalis. The stage when a caterpillar changes into an adult is called a pupa. This change of body shape is called metamorphosis. It takes a monarch butterfly about 10 days to turn into an adult. Other butterflies can take months to change into adults.

## Changing into an Adult

P7 When a pupa has changed into an adult butterfly, the shell around it splits open. It slowly comes out of the shell. The adult butterfly's wings are soft and damp at first. It has to wait a few hours for its wings to dry and its body to get harder. Like all insects, an adult butterfly has three body parts. These are the head, the thorax, and the abdomen. On a butterfly's head there are two eyes and two antennae, which it uses to smell food. In its mouth is a long tube called a proboscis, which it uses to suck up food.

## Mating

P8 The butterfly looks for a mate, so they can continue the life story. Together they can reproduce and create new butterflies.

**Name:** _____

# Life Story of a Butterfly
## Sequence Graphic Organizer

Draw a picture or add a description in each box to show the life story of a butterfly.

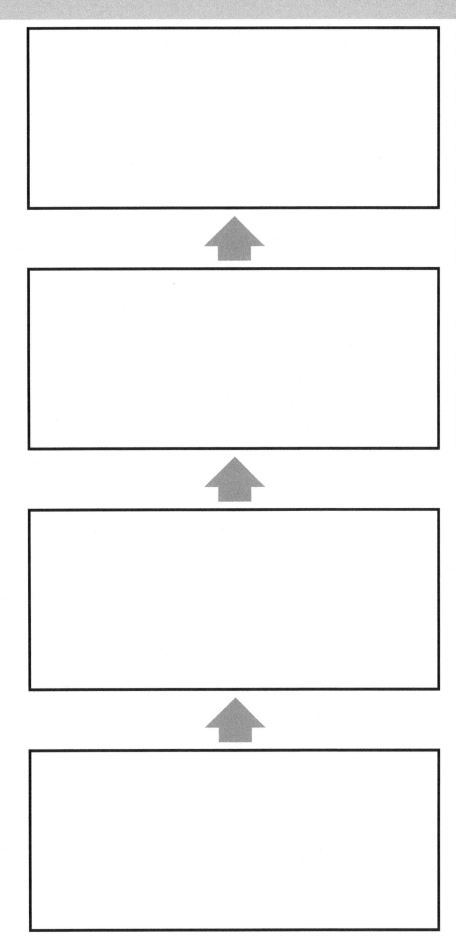

# Beetles

By Rebecca Rissman, published by Heinemann-Raintree

**L1** Do you see that insect crawling on the ground?

**L2** It's a shiny beetle! Look at what we've found.

**L3** What about this green beetle? Can you see it over there?

**L4** Its wings are strong and shiny, to keep it in the air.

**L5** Are all beetles the same color? What colors have you seen?

**L6** Some are black, or red, or blue, and some are even green!

**L7** Look at this black beetle. It's swimming in a puddle.

**L8** Can you see its trail of tiny floating bubbles!

**L9** Beetles can be different, but some things are always true.

**L10** Beetles have six legs. And antennae?
They have two.

**L11** How many body parts do beetles have?
How many can you see?

**L12** Let's count them together: 1, 2, 3!

**L13** Where can you find beetles? Look up, down,
here, and there.

**L14** Beetles are clever bugs. They can live
almost anywhere.

**L15** Baby beetles, called larvae, don't look like their
dad or mom.

**L16** But beetles look more like their parents the older
they become.

**L17** What do beetles eat, when they're crawling
through the weeds?

**L18** They eat other bugs and plants, and sometimes
even seeds!

# Name: _____

## Beetles
### Description Graphic Organizer

Write the word "beetle" in the circle in the middle. In the circles connected to the middle circle, write descriptive words from the text to describe the beetle.

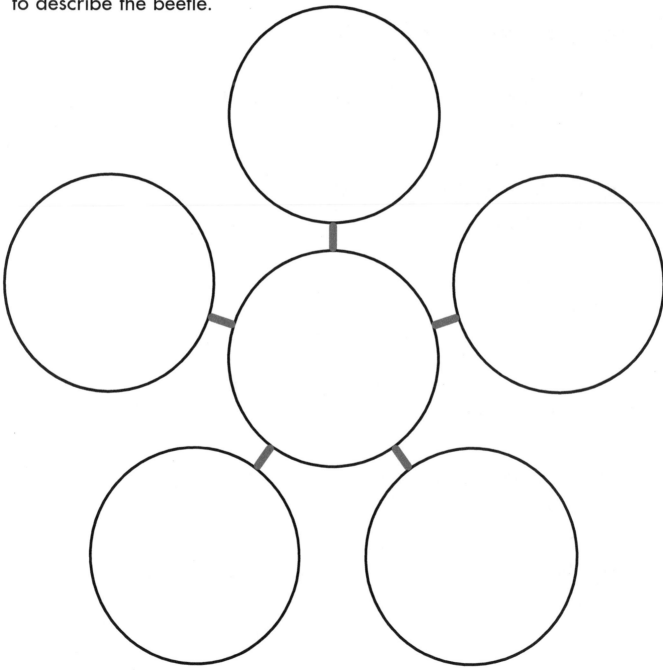

# Sharks

By Megan Cooley Peterson, published by Capstone

## Teeth and Jaws

**P1** Chomp! Sharks have sharp teeth and strong jaws. They use them to catch **prey**.

**P2** When sharks **attack**, their jaws pull away from the skull. A shark is able to open its mouth very wide to bite **prey**.

**P3** When a shark's tooth wears out, a new tooth moves in to replace it. Some sharks go through as many as 30,000 teeth in their lifetime.

**P4** Horn sharks crush the shells of shellfish with their flat back teeth.

## Speedy Swimmers

**P5** Swoosh! Sharks move their heads from side to side when they swim. Sharks can't swim backward.

**P6** A shark's skeleton is made of **cartilage** instead of bone. Flexible cartilage makes swimming easier. Your nose and ears are also made of cartilage.

## Skin and Scales

**P7** Tiny scales called **denticles** cover a shark's skin. Denticles look like small teeth. They make a shark's skin feel like sandpaper.

**P8** Denticles come in many shapes and sizes. They act like armor to protect sharks. Water flows smoothly over denticles, which help sharks swim fast.

# Name: _____

## Sharks
### Description Graphic Organizer

Write the word "shark" in the circle in the middle. In the circles connected to the middle circle, write descriptive words from the text to describe a shark.

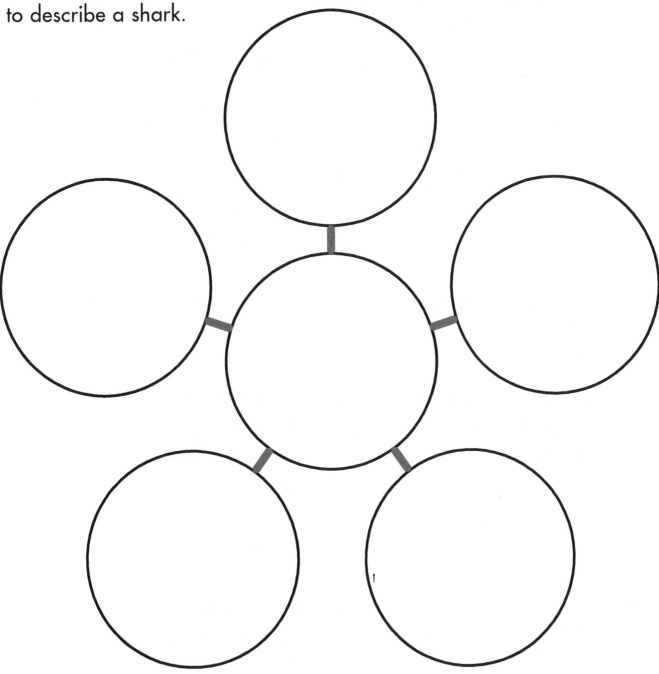

# What Is It? Moth or Butterfly?

By Jill Erfourth, Theresa Hasenauer, and Lorri Zieleniewski

**P1** Suppose a beautiful insect lands on your arm while you are outside. You see six legs and two antennae, and it has wings. You know it's either a moth or a butterfly. But which is it? Butterflies and moths have a lot in common. They both have 6 legs. They both have wings. They also start out the same way, as caterpillars. A butterfly and a moth both go through a big transformation before becoming flying adults!

**P2** So what makes them different? First of all, moths are **nocturnal,** or come out at night. On the other hand, butterflies come out during the day. Moths are also different in that they form a cocoon around themselves, and butterflies form a chrysalis around themselves.

**P3** Butterflies are usually more colorful than moths and have a thin, smooth body. Moths are different because they have thick, fuzzy bodies. Their antennae differ as well. The antennae on a butterfly are long and wider at the end, while a moth's antennae are thin and like a feather.

**P4** These differences are sure to make it easier to decide whether an insect is a moth or a butterfly!

**Name:** _____

# What Is It? Moth or Butterfly
## Venn Diagram

Write the word "moth" on the line above the left circle. Write the word "butterfly" on the line above the right circle. Use information from the text to write the similarities in the middle of the two circles and the differences beneath each insect name.

_____     _____

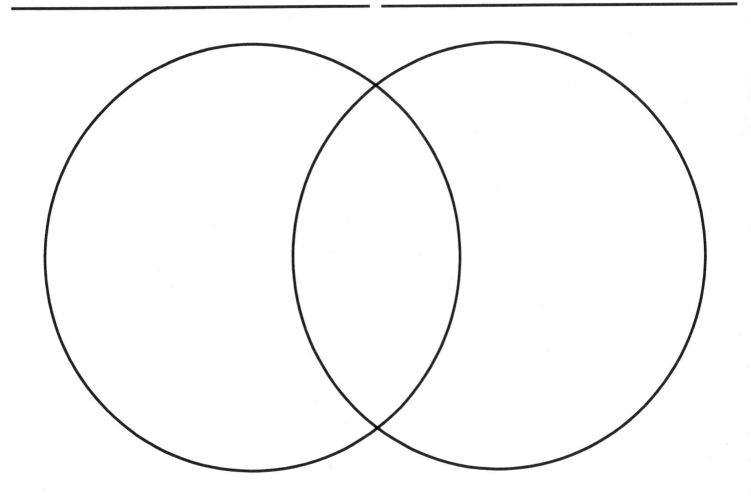

# Year-round School or Traditional School?

By Jill Erfourth, Theresa Hasenauer, and Lorri Zieleniewski

**P1** Wait...I thought there was no school in July or August! We have to go to school in the summer? Schools across the country are switching their traditional nine-month calendars to a year-round calendar for many reasons. While both schedules provide children a great learning opportunity, they have their educational differences.

**P2** ## Year-round School

A year-round calendar does not have an extended summer vacation but rather shorter breaks throughout the year. Students get to enjoy time off in every season. It has benefits to students, such as avoiding the "summer slide" upon returning to school. They won't forget material they've learned. Also, the lazy days of summer eventually get pretty boring, so going to school actually gives kids something to do.

**P3** ## Traditional Nine-month Calendar

In **contrast,** the traditional school year was designed around a nine-month school year with almost three months off in the summer. But did you know that the original purpose of the traditional school calendar with extended summer vacation was to allow children to harvest the crops on the farms? This is hardly the case now. However, if children go to school in the summer, then they have less time to play in the warm weather and less time to splash around in pools. Instead of attending action-packed summer camps where kids can explore their talents and interests, children would be attending school to continue their learning. Year-round school could put a damper on vacation plans for many families who often plan trips during the summer months.

**P4** Both school calendars have a great deal to offer students! After carefully comparing the advantages and disadvantages, would you like to go to school all year-round?

**Name:** _____

# Year-round School or Traditional School?
## Venn Diagram

Write the words "year-round school" on the lines above the left circle.
Write the words "traditional school" on the lines above the right circle.
Use information from the text to write the similarities in the middle of
the two circles and the differences beneath each type of school.

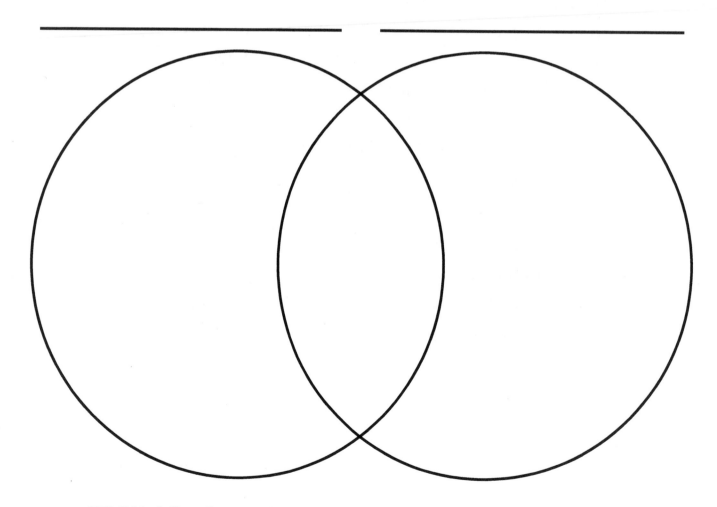

# Wash Those Germs Away!

By Jill Erfourth, Theresa Hasenauer, Lorri Zieleniewski

L1   Our bodies are awesome!

L2   Did you know pesky intruders try to get in our bodies and make us sick?

L3   Those intruders are called germs.

L4   Washing your hands is one of the best ways to stop the spread of germs.

L5   Germs like to snuggle inside your body and cause you to get sick.

L6   Blah!

L7   If you don't wash your hands a lot, then you can pick up germs that can enter your body and make you feel horrible.

L8   By rubbing your eyes, nose or mouth with germy hands that haven't been washed, you can make yourself and your whole family sick!

L9   So if you see friends sneezing or coughing into their hands, remind them to go wash their hands!

L10   You don't want to get sick, do you?

## Name: _____

# Wash Those Germs Away!
## Cause/Effect Graphic Organizer

Use text evidence to write the cause-and-effect relationship in the boxes below.

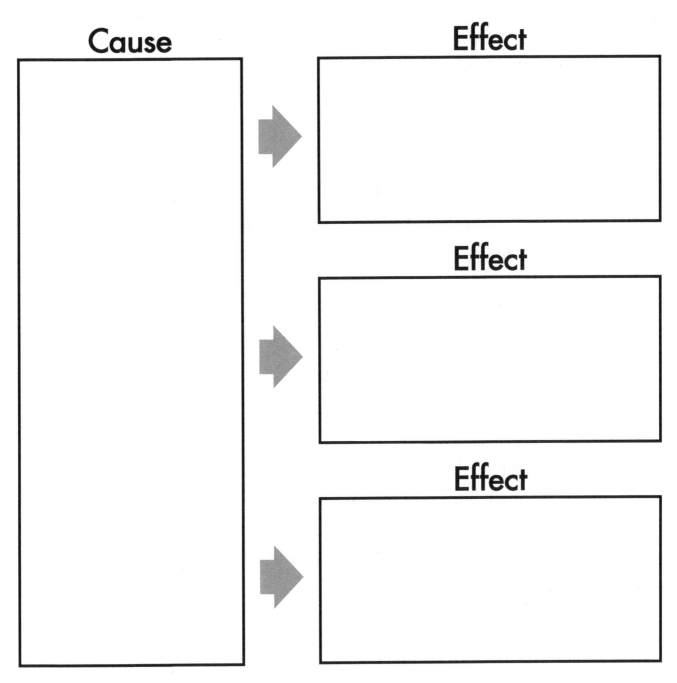

### Cause

### Effect

### Effect

### Effect

# Three Cheers for Trees! A Book about Our Carbon Footprint

By Angie LePetit, published by Capstone

**P1** Every step you take on a beach leaves behind a footprint. So do wet steps on a dry sidewalk or a trek through a muddy yard. Your footprints change the places that you go. But what does a carbon footprint do?

**P2** A carbon footprint doesn't look like a foot. In fact, you can't see it at all! But it is a mark you leave behind. A carbon footprint measures how much you change Earth by using its fossil fuel energy.

**P3** Coal, oil, and natural gas are fossil fuels. They are found deep inside Earth. They have given us energy for many years. But once we use them up, they will be gone forever.

**P4** A hot, polluted planet isn't good for anyone. That's why we need to make good choices about our energy use. The smaller our carbon footprints, the healthier we keep Earth.

**P5** It takes energy to make stuff. An easy way to shrink your carbon footprint is to reuse items. Old socks can be made into puppets. Empty jelly jars make great piggy banks. By reusing items, we keep factories from making too much stuff. It keeps Earth clean too!

**P6** A big part of our carbon footprint comes from driving. Cars, buses, and trucks add a lot of pollution to the air. You can keep Earth cooler and cleaner by walking or riding your bike.

**P7** Lights off! You can reduce your carbon footprint by using less electricity at home. Remember to turn off lights and TVs when they're not in use. In the summer, ask an adult if you can turn up the thermostat a few degrees. In the winter, turn it down.

**P8** There is something else that can help us use less electricity. Can you guess what? TREES! In summer trees shade our homes and keep them cool. In winter trees help keep our homes warm by blocking cold winds.

**P9** Trees are also needed to clean the air. They suck up the gas that makes Earth hot. Then trees give us oxygen to breathe. When too much gas is put in the air, trees can't keep up. This is why we need to use fewer fossil fuels. One tree makes enough oxygen for two people to breathe. Let's plant more trees!

**P10** Trees preserve life. Without them Earth would overheat. And we'd have nothing to breathe! Let's be mindful of what we use and do to take care of our planet. A smaller carbon footprint means a happier home for us all.

# Name: _____

## Three Cheers for Trees!
### Cause/Effect Graphic Organizer

Use text evidence to write the cause-and-effect relationship in the boxes below.

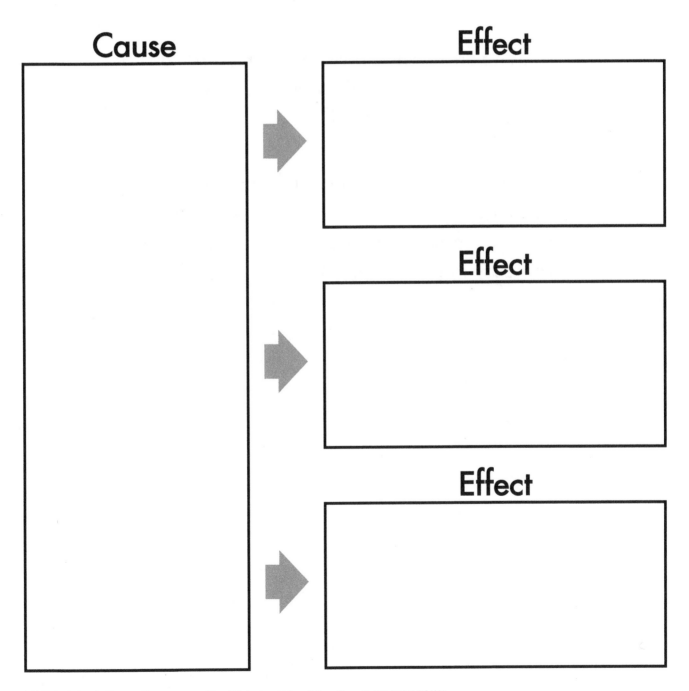

**Cause**

**Effect**

**Effect**

**Effect**

# A Sticky Idea

Published by ReadWorks.org: The Solution to Reading Comprehension.

**P1** Have you ever put a sticky bandage on a cut? The best-known sticky bandages are called Band-Aids. They were invented in 1920.

**P2** A man named Earle Dickson invented Band-Aids. Earle wanted to help his wife. She often cut her fingers when she cooked.

**P3** At the time, people had to make their own bandages. They cut pieces of gauze and tape. Those bandages were hard to use. Earle's idea was easy to use. Thanks, Earle!

**Name:** _____

# A Sticky Idea
Problem/Solution Graphic Organizer

Use evidence from the text to write or draw the problem and solution in the boxes below.

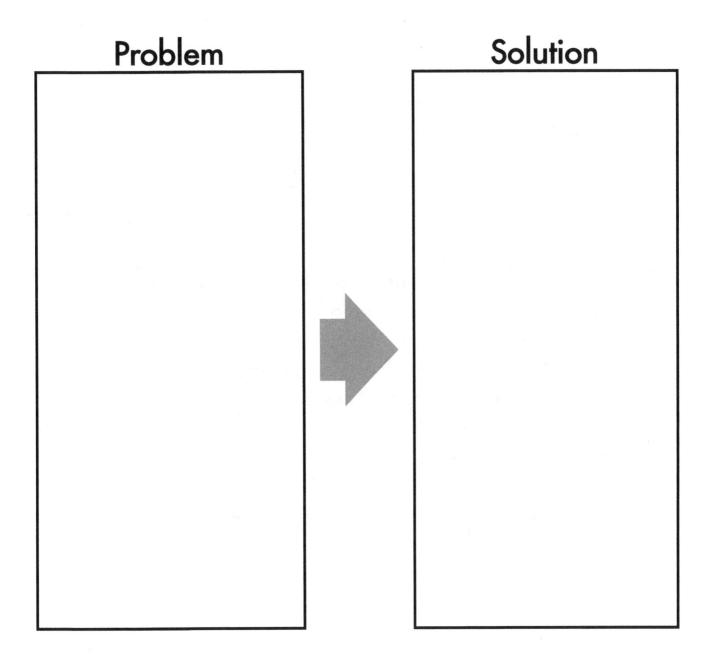

| Problem | Solution |
|---------|----------|

# Trash Magic: A Book about Recycling a Plastic Bottle

By Angie LePetit, published by Capstone

**P1** Gulp! It's easy to grab a bottle of water, juice, or soda when you are thirsty. But where do all those bottles come from? And why is it so important to recycle them? Let's find out!

**P2** To make a plastic bottle, you start with oil—a dark, sticky fossil fuel. Machines called oil rigs drill for oil deep in the earth. Long, strawlike pipes suck the oil out of the ground.

**P3** Making plastic from oil takes a lot of work. First, the oil must be cleaned and heated. When it's really hot, chemicals are added, and the oil thickens. As it cools, the oil turns into little crumbs called raw plastic. Raw plastic doesn't look like much. That's because it needs to get heated again. The crumbs melt together, and more chemicals are added. As the new plastic cools, it becomes stretchy. Blow air into the stretchy plastic, and you have a bottle!

P4 It takes a lot of work and natural resources to make a plastic bottle, and millions are used every day. It's too bad not all of them get recycled. Some get tossed to the roadside as litter. Others end up in the ocean. Even more are put in the garbage and dumped in landfills.

P5 Here's the problem—plastic does not easily fall apart. Remember the chemicals used to make the plastic? It takes hundreds of years for them to leave the bottles. Once they do, the chemicals soak into the ground. They can get into our water, which is not safe. Drinking these chemicals makes you sick.

P6 There's another reason to recycle plastic bottles. Do you remember what dark and sticky liquid makes plastic? That's right: oil. And where does oil come from? Right again: the ground. If we use oil too fast, we could run out.

P7 So what can you do with an empty plastic bottle? You could wash it and reuse it. Or you could recycle it. If you want to recycle the bottle, place the bottle in a recycling bin. It's that easy!

**Name:** _____

# Trash Magic: A Book about Recycling a Plastic Bottle
## Problem/Solution Graphic Organizer

Use evidence from the text to write the problem and solution in the boxes below.

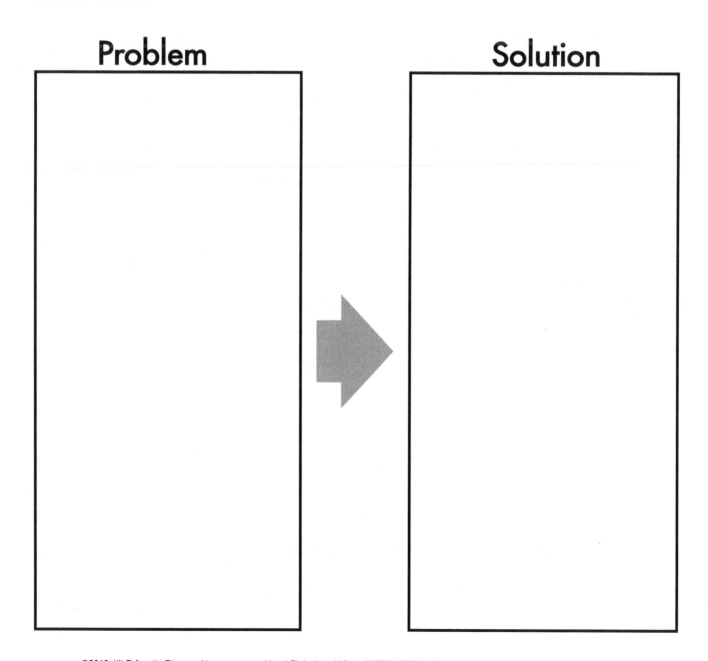

## Problem

## Solution

**Name:** _____

# Sequencing Paragraph Frame

Title: _____

This text tells the sequence of _____ ,

First, _____

_____

Second, _____

_____

Next, _____

_____

Finally, _____

_____

**Name:** _____

# Description Paragraph Frame

Title: _____

Topic Sentence: _____

_____

Body: (1st detail) _____

_____

(2nd detail) _____

_____

(3rd detail) _____

_____

Conclusion: _____

_____

**Name:** _____

# Compare/Contrast Paragraph Frame

_____ and _____ are similar

in several ways. First, _____

and _____ .

They also _____

_____ . Because of these similarities,

_____ .

There are some differences between _____ and

_____ as well. One way they differ is _____

_____ .

Another way they differ is _____

(Concluding sentence) _____

_____ .

**Name:** _____

# Cause/Effect Paragraph Frame

_____ happens because of

_____ .

As a result, _____

_____ .

Therefore, _____

_____ .

This explains why _____

_____ .

# Name: _____

# Problem/Solution Paragraph Frame

The problem is _____

_____.

As a result, _____

_____ happened.

# Name: _____

# Respond to Reading:
## The Four Essential Questions of Close and Critical Reading

| Question 1 — What does the text say? | Question 2 — How does the text say it? |
|---|---|
| • What are the key ideas in the text?<br><br>• What is the summary or gist? | • How is the text organized? What is the text structure?<br><br>• Author's craft: genre, organizations, text features, word choice, figures of speech, punctuation, etc. |
| | |

# Respond to Reading:
## The Four Essential Questions of Close and Critical Reading

| Question 3 — What does the text mean? | Question 4 — What does it mean to my life? |
|---|---|
| • What is the message of the text?<br>• What does the author believe? | • Text-to-text connections<br>• Text-to-self connections<br>• Text-to-world connections |
| | |

# The Four Essential Questions of Close and Critical Reading

| Essential Question 1:<br><br>What does the text say? | Essential Question 2:<br><br>How does the text say it? | Essential Question 3:<br><br>What does the text mean? | Essential Question 4:<br><br>What does it mean to my life? |
|---|---|---|---|
| Summarize the text containing the key details. CC1, CC2<br><br>What is the main topic of the text? CC1, CC2<br><br>Retell the key ideas of the text. CC2<br><br>What is the specific textual evidence (facts that can be proven with evidence) used to support the main topic? CC1<br><br>What are the most important ideas/events? CC1, CC2<br><br>What are the ideas in order of importance or presentation? CC1 | How is the information organized (e.g., sequence, compare/contrast, cause/effect, description, problem/solution)? CC5<br><br>What are the text features (title, headings, illustrations, captions, index, glossary, chapter, etc.)? CC5<br><br>Whose voice did the author choose as narrator? CC3<br><br>What role does dialogue play in the text? CC3<br><br>What word choice, imagery, vocabulary, and figures of speech (e.g., simile, metaphor, alliteration, irony, repetition, personification, etc.) does the author use? CC4 | What is the central idea or theme of the text? CC2<br><br>How does the author support the central idea or theme with ideas and details? CC2<br><br>Identify the main purpose of a text, including what the author wants to answer, explain, or describe. CC6 | **Text(s)-to-self: CC7**<br><br>What does this remind me of in my life?<br><br>What is this similar/different to in my life?<br><br>Has something like this ever happened to me?<br><br>How does this relate to my life?<br><br>**Text(s)-to-text: CC9**<br><br>What does this remind me of in another book I've read?<br><br>How is this text similar/different to other things I've read?<br><br>Have I read about something like this before?<br><br>**Text(s)-to-world: CC7**<br><br>What does this remind me of in the real world?<br><br>How is this text similar and/or different from things that happen in the real world? |

CC designations refer to standards from Common Core College and Career Readiness Anchor Standards for Reading.

Adapted *from Guided Highlighted Reading* by Weber, Schofield, and Nelson (Maupin House, 2012)

# REFERENCES

# WORKS CITED

Akhondi, Masoumeh, Faramarz Aziz Malayeri, and Abd Arshad Samad. "How to Teach Expository Text Structure to Facilitate Reading Comprehension." *The Reading Teacher*, 64: pp. 368–372. doi: 10.1598/RT.64.5.9, 2011.

Beck, Isabel L., Margaret G. McKeown, and Linda Kucan. *Bringing Words to Life: Robust Vocabulary Instruction*. New York: Guilford, 2002.

Beck, Isabel L., Margaret G. McKeown, and Linda Kucan. *Creating Robust Vocabulary: Frequently Asked Questions and Extended Examples*. New York: Guilford, 2008.

*Evidence-based Reading Instruction: Putting the National Reading Panel Report into Practice*. Newark, DE: International Reading Association, 2002.

Goldman, S.R. & J.A. Rakestraw. (2000). "Structural Aspects of Constructing Meaning from Text." In M. L. Kamil, P. B. Mosenthal, P. D. Pearson, & R. Barr (Eds.), *Handbook of Reading Research* (Vol. 3, pp. 311–336). Mahwah, NJ: Erlbaum.

Marzano, Robert J. "Marzano Research | Home." Accessed August 19, 2014. http://www.marzanoresearch.com.

Pearson, P. D. & N.K. Duke. (2002). "Comprehension Instruction in the Primary Grades." In C. C. Block & M. Pressley (Eds.), *Comprehension Instruction: Research-based Best Practices* (pp. 247–258). New York: Guilford.

Pearson, P. David, Rebecca Barr, Michael L. Kamil, and Peter Mosenthal. *Handbook of Reading Research*. New York: Longman, 1984–2011.

Ritchhart, Ron, Mark Church, and Karin Morrison. *Making Thinking Visible: How to Promote Engagement, Understanding, and Independence for All Learners*. San Francisco, CA: Jossey-Bass, 2011.

Swanson, H. Lee, Karen R. Harris, and Steve Graham. *Handbook of Learning Disabilities*. New York: Guilford Press, 2003.

Weber, Elaine M., Barbara A. Nelson, and Cynthia Lynn Schofield. *Guided Highlighted Reading: A Close-reading Strategy for Navigating Complex Text*. Gainesville, FL: Maupin House Pub., 2012.

# MENTOR TEXTS

"A Sticky Idea." ReadWorks.org: The Solution to Reading Comprehension. Accessed December 18, 2014. http://www.readworks.org/passages/sticky-idea.

Guillain, Charlotte. *Life Story of a Butterfly*. Chicago, IL: Heinemann-Raintree, 2015.

"How Plastic Is Recycled." ReadWorks.org: The Solution to Reading Comprehension. Accessed December 18, 2014. http://www.readworks.org/passages/how-plastic-recycled.

LePetit, Angie. *Three Cheers for Trees! A Book about Our Carbon Footprint*. North Mankato, MN: Capstone, 2013.

LePetit, Angie. *Trash Magic: A Book about Recycling a Plastic Bottle*. North Mankato, MN: Capstone, 2013.

Peterson, Megan Cooley. *Sharks*. North Mankato, MN: Capstone, 2014.

Rissman, Rebecca. *Beetles*. Chicago, IL: Heinemann-Raintree, 2013.

Maupin House *by*
# capstone
professional

At Maupin House by Capstone Professional, we continue to look for professional development resources that support grades K–8 classroom teachers in areas, such as these:

| | |
|---|---|
| **Literacy** | **Language Arts** |
| **Content-Area Literacy** | **Research-Based Practices** |
| **Assessment** | **Inquiry** |
| **Technology** | **Differentiation** |
| **Standards-Based Instruction** | **School Safety** |
| **Classroom Management** | **School Community** |

If you have an idea for a professional development resource, visit our Become an Author website at:

http://maupinhouse.com/index.php/become-an-author

There are two ways to submit questions and proposals.

1. You may send them electronically to:

http://maupinhouse.com/index.php/become-an-author

2. You may send them via postal mail. Please be sure to include a self-addressed stamped envelope for us to return materials.

**Acquisitions Editor**
**Capstone Professional**
**1 N. LaSalle Street, Suite 1800**
**Chicago, IL 60602**